AF680481

JULIANA JONES

HEDGED

First published by CG HOLDINGS 2022

First edition

ISBN: 979-8-9853224-0-8

This book was professionally typeset on Reedsy.
Find out more at reedsy.com

This is written for every trader out there
Who has ever lost money in the market.
I've been there.

* * *

And for Marc.
Who knew everything...
Yet nothing at all.

* * *

Five percent of all net proceeds of this book will be donated to Breast Cancer Alliance in honor of my favorite author, Jackie Collins.
RIP, Jackie. I love you.

"There is in every one of us, even those who seem to be most moderate, a type of desire that is terrible, wild, and lawless."
— Plato, The Republic

"The mind of a trader... highly intelligent. And if you can beat the market, you're f*cking brilliant."
— Ex-Trader, 7 years in prison

"A gambler with a system must be, to a greater or lesser extent, insane."
— George Augustus Sala

1

Chapter 1

I wanted to stop. I didn't want to do it. But I was lying in bed… and I couldn't help myself. The craving arrives, it overwhelms me…

It comes without warning… and I'm in it again.

Oh, God, it feels *so good.* This position.

This is it… this *is it.*

Don't stop... don't stop. That's it, keep going...

I'm elated. I'm in ecstasy. I need more. Much more. I'm in over my head again. I'm in way too deep… but I can't stop myself.

I won't.

I don't need to, my other side argues.

You've got this.

You 100% got this.

I stare straight ahead. My eyes hold a dangerous gleam. My senses are all heightened; everything takes on a visceral sense. I am in another state, another world, another mind. My heart races and its good today. So *good.*

My cat, Sam, enters my bedroom. He jumps on my desk and sits beside me, erect and kingly.

I grab my mouse and it falls into my hand as easily as the apple Adam took from Eve, and I click and click, buying more and more.

I'm sitting in front of six computer screens… and I'm day trading. I'm in a Chinese stock tied to cryptocurrency: SOS and it's going higher… *and higher.*

I bought in way too high days ago, and it had plummeted. I was going to leave it alone, let it ride, not sell out of my other positions, but I had to.

Because if I averaged down and bought more, I would make more… *eventually... when it popped.*

And boy, was it about to!

It just broke out of a descending channel and hit a new weekly high. The stock was still hammered; I managed to get my account back up to $211,000 from $25,000 when I blew up trading Apple options. What a nightmare that was.

But I came back.

Because I always come back.

I'm a trader.

A fucking trader.

I can, and do, beat the market on a daily basis.

And today will be no different.

Today I will win.

Because that's what it's all about: winning.

And I'll always be a winner.

My finger twitches… I hit the keys… stocks flash in green and red, a dizzying narcotic blur of columns and numbers. Warp speed… Everything's a blur. The blinds are closed; there are no reminders that a real world of duty or drudgery exists beyond my seductive cocoon.

Assurance and wisdom fill my enormous green eyes with radiant luminosity as the stock ticks up.

The phone rings. *Ignore it,* I tell myself. I'm too close now…

On the fourth ring, I hear it: "Jolette, it's Paul. I've left you four messages. Will you ever call back?"

I see a spider walking across the cover of my FORTUNE magazine. I lift the magazine, carry it over to the open window, and set the spider free.

On the cover is a large photo of hedge fund extraordinaire Steven Benson staring right back at me. The article asks: "Manipulator or Visionary?" I stare at Steve Benson's photo more intently. He's perfectly coiffed with a king-of-the-world smile. *I'd give anything to work for him someday*.

Sitting back down at my desk, I reach for my red bandana and wrap it around my forehead. I study charts assiduously. My heart pounds with increasing speed. Adrenaline burns through my bloodstream.

I check the stock message boards: From TexasTrader12: "I am out with my girl and saw the price. My boner exploded through my pants and knocked over the table." From BlockChainStar: "Hold til 80! Don't sell!" with the stupid Leonardo DiCaprio GIF from the *Wolf of Wall Street.*

I turn to the chart again. And I'm astonished that one can make this fast, this easily, this much money with the click of a mouse.

I start to click and unload the shares as the stock goes higher and higher, clicking and screaming, "OHHHHHHH YESSSSSSS!!!"

Selling into the momentum, I keep going. "YES! YESSSS! *YESSSSSS*! And a glorious message pops up on my screen: "You sold 8,800 shares of SOS at $9.03, net profit +$15,654."

I'm manic, euphoric, orgasmic!

"We did it, Sammy!" Jumping out of my chair, wearing short-shorts and a white T-shirt, I kiss my cat on my desk and twirl around! "FIFTEEN GRAND IN THE BAG!"

"That's fifteen thousand, not fifteen hundred, Sammy – fifteen THOUSAND DOLLARSSSS!"

Sitting back down in my chair, I stare at my screens, contemplating my next trade.

I'm lost in a high so incredible, I will chase it again and again for all the rest of my days.

I check the chart of Bed Bath and Beyond. It looks delicious. I back up the truck and buy in. A tasty 7,000 shares.

I also see a new trending cryptocurrency, Vechain. Also looks juicy. I buy in. It's only .12 cents so I can buy hundreds of thousands of coins.

Let's go…

Making one dollar is too many.

Making fifteen thousand is never enough.

Bring it!

2

Chapter 2

I burst into the air doing a 10 foot wheelie on my mountain bicycle ignoring the warning signs that read: DANGER: MEN WORKING!

I land on the ground with a BAMMMMM and grin and speed up like a madwoman.

Riding my bike with my childhood friend, Brittany, we're cutting corners at unprecedented speed, racing each other through Pacific Heights. We're both twenty-seven years old and have been best friends since we were five.

Careening around a corner, we blow through a stop sign, blazing down another hill, almost missing a parked car.

I brake in front of a traffic light, not even bothering to unhook my custom Sidi's from the pedals. I maintain the bike in perfect, stationary balance. Just the right height for two guys in business suits in a BMW convertible to admire the results of my workout regimen.

"We're long a million shares of Rip."

Overhearing this, I turn to them with ecstatic eyes. "It's a short... Check out the new currency Dragonchain."

"Huh?"

"Buy 300,000. Sit on it a week or two. Then blow out when it hits 490." I crack a smile. They're impressed.

The light turns green and I tear off down the windy street. "Hey, wait a minute!"

But I'm gone.

I swerve between two cars with six inches to spare, hedging it *with pure precision.*

* * *

Brittany and I ride until we reach our final destination, the Clipper Yacht Club, the most prestigious marina in the San Francisco Bay area. Home of many fine boats and yachts, this exclusive club has an illustrious array of visiting motor yachts, housing eight hundred slips.

Brittany jumps off her bike and puts her arm around me. "You always win, Jolette," she says, out of breath.

Inwardly, I grin, but I don't rub it in. "Lunch is on me, my friend…"

* * *

The crowd on the Yacht Club balcony is young, restless, and loud. A live band plays in the corner. We devour three plates of shrimp and grilled vegetables, and I'm still hungry. "I want steak, Britt."

"That's not on the menu for team triathlon training. Fish, vegetables, and plenty of carbs."

"Are we really going to do this?"

"Yep. This is going to be our year to win it!" Putting another shrimp in her mouth, she washes it down with a glass of Evian.

"The Triathlon, Brittany? You know I don't like being on a team, even if it's just for training."

"It'll be fine. We're going to do great!"

Her face lights up and I can't help but love her enthusiasm. Brittany's a cool, willowy blonde with classic style and an aspiring model. Her aquamarine eyes compliment her fine porcelain skin and perfect bone structure.

"So what's happening with your job, are they offering you any covers?"

She nods.

"Wow, Britt, that's great! Congratulations. Why didn't you say something?"

"It's just a call back. I don't think I'll get it."

"You'll get it."

"You really think so?" she asks lightly.

"Of course you will. Why wouldn't you?" I assure her, wiping my hands on a napkin.

"You're right, but if they don't call, should I call them?"

"They'll call," I say, and lean back in my chair. My gaze shifts to the Arioso; a huge, opulent mega-yacht with helipad, a glass encased swimming pool, and a triumph of amenities. "I want my father to upgrade to that."

"Your father's houseboat is perfectly fine. Humble, yet charming in its own way. How's he doing?" she asks, carefully. "Are you still worried?"

I put my sunglasses on and take a sip of my iced coffee, nodding.

"You haven't slept, have you?"

"Been up the past forty-eight hours trading."

"Gee-sus. Help your father then. You're good at what you do."

"He doesn't believe in me."

Brittany turns and looks over the crowd. "Oh great, Paul Zucker's here."

I look over at his table. He's sitting with a group of five hedge fund managers, cocky and rowdy. He's a prominent Wall Street analyst known for his arrogance and tailored suits, but everything he makes goes right up his nose.

"He despises you, you know that?" Brittany acknowledges.

"...Now there's a heartbreaker."

"What did you do to him?" she asks, raising a perfectly groomed eyebrow.

"I don't even remember."

I turn to Paul. His shrewd eyes are assessing and bear into mine. He raises his glass to mine. Smart and calculating, he possesses Ivy League mannerisms and his perfectionism runs deep.

"If only I had the chance, Britt, I could do what they do, only better."

"You can't take a balance sheet to bed with you, Jolette."

"Wanna bet?"

The blades of a helicopter slice the wind making a loud TICK. TICK. TICK. sound, blowing our hair, and making it impossible to hear.

A Bell-Boeing 609 tiltrotor appears in the sky. It hovers over the Arioso and lands on its helipad.

We watch as the doors open, and a perfectly groomed man in a Caraceni business suit steps off. He's thirty years old and stunning. Electric blue eyes radiate effortless confidence. He walks onto the yacht.

"Now there's a heartbreaker..." Brittany says dreamily.

He has blonde hair parted to the side, an athletic body, and expensive good looks. He deftly makes his way through the crowd, reading his cell phone.

Bikini-clad bodies, oiled and gleaming, lie by the Arioso pool, and look up at him. A Slavic blonde, with cheekbones that could slice butter, shoots him a long look. Russian Oligarchs, Kuwaiti Royals, and other global jet-setters sip cocktails and survey him.

"Who's that?" I ask.

"Noel Sheffield. A killer Wall Street broker in his prime. Cultured.

Charming. Troubled. Dangerous... "

We sit in contented silence watching him.

"He's a risk taker and a heart breaker. Dated some models I work with. I have to get myself a boyfriend..." Brittany admits.

"Relationships – they're like money, easier made then kept." I take out a roll of cash and signal for the waitress. "I have to go. My father's birthday party's at four. Are you sure you can't come by?"

"I have that fitting at four thirty. Will your brother be there?"

"Probably," I reply, and rise from my chair. "Stay here then, enjoy dessert."

"I shouldn't."

"You should."

"Thanks, Jolette. And don't forget, first day of practice is Wednesday, 5:00 a.m. You'll be there, right?"

"Yes..." I say, manufacturing a smile.

I get up exposed to every stare, but my eyes remain solely fixed on The Arioso... *and Noel Sheffield.*

* * *

I see Paul Zucker standing outside in front of my bike. He's talking with someone in a heated manner... Someone I only see the back of.

"What happened?" the guy asks.

"No, that's the first thing I asked him. He came back from New York, empty. Benson didn't buy in!"

"Where is he?"

"Yeah, he's there. I mean, you're on this, Noel, right? The clients I have in Sequenom – We need Benson!"

I check my watch and can't be late for my father. I walk closer, and as I approach them, I see Paul's talking to *Noel Sheffield.*

"All right, I'll take care of it," Noel says.

They see me and freeze with their mouths gaped open.

"Excuse me."

They move aside, and I pull my bike out of the stand.

I jump on it and take off, catching eyes with Noel Sheffield, and my heart skips a beat.

3

Chapter 3

Arriving at the smallest slip in the smallest marina in Sausalito, I chain my bike to a lamp post.

The soft sound of the clanging sails and seagulls calling from above relaxes me, and the waterfront is naturally peaceful. Looking across the scalloped harbor, I take in the panoramic view of Mount Tamalpais and its hillside homes. They're so discretely nestled against a beautiful green backdrop, it looks like a scene from a postcard.

My adorable eight year old twin nephews, Devin and Dan, sit on the dock, dangling their feet in the water. When they see me coming, they get up and charge towards me. "Aunt Jolette's here!"

I bend down and they hurl themselves into my arms. "How are my sweet princes?!" I ask, smothering them with kisses. They're so cute with their white blonde hair and matching navy blue polo shirts.

Reaching into my jacket pocket, I pull out some candy. "Guess what I brought for you?"

"Crunch bars?!" Devin guesses.

"Yep!" I hand them each their favorite treat.

"Thank you. Do you want to see our magic trick?" Dan asks.

"Sure."

He pulls out a stack of cards. "Now I'm gonna make all these disappear."

The twins go into hocus pocus theatrics and Dan shakes his hand wildly. The cards go flying, the trick doesn't pan out.

I take their cards and begin a magic trick. The twins watch spellbound. "Now where's your card?" I ask, having fun with them.

Devin points to a card.

"Are you sure?"

He nods. I release the card and they're wrong. "Remember, it's never as it appears."

They laugh and take their back cards. We start to walk to my father's houseboat and Devin reminds me, "You're still coming to our Career Day, right Aunt Jolette? You promised you'd talk about the stock market."

"Yes, yes, of course. Anything you need. When is it?"

"November 17."

I make a mental note to write it down in my calendar. "I won't forget."

My stomach tightens in knots as we get closer to my father's houseboat. A new coat of brown paint can't hide the numbers of years on it.

I have a plan. I don't want him to worry about anything.

And I hope it works.

* * *

"Happy birthday to you...Happy birthday...dear Dad... happy birthday to youuuuu!"

Sarah, my older sister, carries the cake. Her husband, Lee, a steady guy who's a math teacher, stands beside her. My brother, Troy, a rebellious jock with a halo of jet black hair, sits in the corner drinking a beer as we all sing happy birthday to my father, the weathered, widower patriarch of our clan.

We had a mother, and then we didn't, and it was that fast.

My father blows out the candles, and smiles. He's a tall, handsome man with a serious and dignified demeanor who's never been consumed by luxury or extravagance. He lives a humble, quiet life on his houseboat and has so for years.

"How does it feel, Dad?" I ask. "The big 6 0?"

"Feels great," he replies. "You look upbeat, Jolette."

"Thank you."

"As bright and sparkly as a brand new penny," he adds.

"Hard work, a clean conscience, and a simple life, Dad." We exchange a look, communicating volumes of admiration. "Did you make a wish?"

He nods. "Peace."

"I have the road map for peace. Financial security. I have some new trading ideas and I'm going to help you. These ideas are going to fly!"

"I think you mean attract flies," Troy pipes in.

"I think it just did."

Troy's hair is swept across his forehead like a tornado and he looks like Elvis Presley. My brother, Troy, the partier and the lady killer. Never loved another person in his whole life. Including himself.

"Troy, we're going to get you the help you need."

"Shut up, Jolette."

"Jolette!" Sarah snaps.

Everyone stops eating. There's no more denying the tension.

* * *

I join my sister in the kitchen, "Troy's drinking again, huh?" The question doesn't need a response.

Troy ran his own investment management company for a while, filed for bankruptcy, and he's been on a downward spiral since. We don't like to talk about him. "You need any help?" I ask.

Her thick brown hair is gleaming and pulled back into a thick bun at the nape of her neck. She rarely wears makeup or jewelry except for the wedding ring on her finger.

"No thanks, I'm good."

Outside the windows, we see our father walking alone on the marina. "Go and talk to Dad."

I squeeze her shoulders affectionately and go outside to join my father.

* * *

The sun's setting. I push my bicycle and walk along beside my father. "How are you sleeping, Dad?"

"Better, thanks. What have you been up to?"

"Today I was over at the Clipper. Had lunch with Brittany."

"Oh, the fancy yacht club… You know I hear they charge two thousand a foot over there? Man, it's just a dock."

"I know, Dad, just a bunch of people just trying to impress each other. Speaking of impressed, you really would be if you knew how good I was doing day trading."

"I am very proud of you."

"But you're making one percent in a CD. I have a dozen of opportunities a day. Of course, I want you to be proud of me, but I want you to take advantage of this too."

"Jolette, remember what happened when I gave that Rothman Securities broker a hundred thousand dollars?"

"Yes, they churned your account and buried you."

My father nods. "And you see what happened to your brother."

"Yes, Dad."

I take in his face and realize that this is the man I've loved my whole life. "Look, I started with twelve thousand dollars and I'm liquid almost a quarter of a million now. I have studied every type of chart, read every book, and understand every kind of economic theory. I've mastered technical *and* fundamental analysis. You have my spreadsheets with my returns, right?"

He nods.

"Next year, I plan on doubling it!"

He's getting excited, I can tell. I keep going. "Cryptocurrency is where it's at right now! Bitcoin is up 7,700 percent in the past five years! I bought Dogecoin at an eighth of a penny and it's up over 8000 percent now. Huge money, Dad! Huuuuge!"

"Look, I have a hundred and eighty-seven thousand dollars left in my savings. Now that I'm alone, that's enough for me. I don't want to gamble it."

"But Dad, you're missing out – on money that you could've made, money that *you need.* Did you take a look at those P&L statements I gave you?"

"Not yet."

I swallow my frustration.

Sarah watches us through the window.

"Jolette, I believe in companies with good fundamentals."

"I do too, Dad. Okay, I have another idea: Bed, Bath and Beyond... They just increased their e-commerce division and spent money on their supply chain. They're targeting low to mid-digits same store sales growth and $1 billion dollars in operating profits."

"Interesting," he agrees.

"They're coming out with earnings on Monday and they're going to blow it out. I already own some shares in my portfolio."

"Sounds good."

"Dad!" Sarah calls from the boat. "Are you out of water?! I'm trying to wash the dishes and no water is coming out of sink!"

"Oh, no," my father stammers.

"Dad, is the boat okay?"

"Jolette, I don't know. I have someone coming to look at it on Monday. I better go back inside and help your sister."

"I'll tell you what, Dad, transfer the funds over to my iTrade account tonight." I pull out my phone, thinking fast, moving fast. "I just emailed you my account numbers. If we buy in before the open, we can ride the pop."

"That sounds great."

He nods and we high five each other. "Yeah!!!"

"This is going to be great, Dad!"

We high five each other again, both elated. "We're going to make a huuuuuge score!!!"

He bends down and kisses me on my forehead."I love you."

"I love you, too, Dad."

4

Chapter 4

Brittany and I dive into the water of an Olympic Size Swimming Pool. A TRIATHLON TRAINING" sign hangs in the corner.

Underwater, I replay my Bed Bath and Beyond trade from earlier this morning. I put every penny of my father's money on it and it bought me 4,590 shares.

4,590 beautiful shares.

My father is going to be extremely happy....

I also bought more stock for my own account. The company's reporting earnings today, and this is going to fly.

Bed, Bath and Beyond, how I love thee. You have been trending up, my friend, and Investors Business Weekly just ranked you as their #1 stock pick. Now show me the money!

On a high, I swim faster and faster, thrusting my legs and body underwater without any bond or connection anywhere; just myself in this watery world. My thin arms chop the water and I lift my head up, swimming faster, and see that I am, indeed, way ahead of the other swimmers. The whistle blows –

"Hey!" the coach yells. "Jolette, you can't join and immediately be number one! It takes *practice*. Everyday, *practice!* Each day, you'll get better, stronger, faster. Your father should have named you, "Patience," so maybe you'd have some!"

People laugh at me. Brittany, who's beside me, also starts laughing. *Someone should have named her brain, so maybe she'd have one,* I want to say, but hold back.

I jump out of the pool and check my phone.

The coach blows the whistle again, "Start over everyone!"

I pull up the Bed, Bath and Beyond stock.

And what I see astonishes me.

The stock is tanking.

BBBY is flashing in RED – DOWN 8 POINTS! I wipe my watery eyes and check again.

It can't be.

Panic surges through me. *What happened?* The stock's DOWN 8 DOLLARS AND FALLING!

Now 9…

Dropping like a stone!

* * *

Panic assails me. My mind swims with confusion. Faster and faster I pedal on my bicycle. I run red lights, barreling through traffic, swerving, skidding, passing cars in traffic with maybe six inches to spare on either side.

This really isn't happening.

Oh no, please no.

I turn a corner wearing ear buds. The music blares so fucking loud. Streetlights smear behind me like neon streamers. The road comes at me at full speed, looks as though it will hit me in the eyes –

Rounding another corner, I don't see the oncoming car… TWO

WORLDS ARE ABOUT TO COLLIDE!

The driver SLAMS ON THE BRAKES!

A LOUD SCREEEEEECH! I SWERVE, SLIDE, GO AIRBORNE – and CRASH to the ground!

Silence.

Pain shoots through me. With a groan, I roll over and try to push myself up. Painfully, I hobble back to my bike. *I need to get home. I only live a few blocks away.*

My entire right forearm is slicked with blood. My limbs are functioning. Nothing seems shattered.

Physically that is.

Financially, it may be a different story.

A woman gets out of her car.

"Hey! Are you —"

But I'm gone.

* * *

Rushing up the stairs, I carry the bike on my shoulder, and race inside. Sitting down at my computers, I type in: BBBY.

The chart displays it's descending straight down. *Not good.* I look at the volume. *It's high. This thing is tanking.*

A scream of panic rises up in my throat. The stock continues to go lower and I stare at my screens open-mouthed, "Holy shit."

My mind is in chaos. I hit the keyboard, trying to buy....Trying to sell....Trying to average down... trying to do anything to stop this bleeding!

My body fills with terror. My heart tightens and I'm besieged by an overpowering fear. A feeling I've never had before.

I average down, adding on more and more shares. But that's known as the "moron trade," piling on more shares to a position that's tanking.

For a second, I think I'm okay.

The stock stabilizes. *Maybe there's a chance.*

Oh, God, please, let there be a chance.

The stock starts to tick up. 02 cents, .14 cents..."Keep going... that's it...." I feel a sense of hope.

But then it shoots down a quarter and goes lower again! Courage deserts me. Losses are multiplying. The old adage runs through my mind: "When you find yourself in a hole – stop digging!"

But I can't.

I can't stop.

I keep buying more shares.

Holy fuck!

Now I'm on margin.

Stop me.

Help me.

Kill me!

I feel wretched. I put my hands up to my face and cry involuntarily, "Oh, no!" I'm stunned, horrified... my universe is coming unglued.

I clutch the desk. *This is a fucking disaster.* I take several deep breaths and screw my eyes tightly shut and utter another silent prayer, desperate and beseeching.

I check the news: "Bed, Bath & Beyond shares dive more than 26% as supply chain issues hit sales, inflation eats into profits..."

I check the stock message boards, "TIMBERRR...Get out! What a nightmare! HOLY FUCK!"

I look back at my screens frozen. It feels as if a knife is cutting at my insides and I'm unable to speak in the searing grief. I'm losing everything.

Oh God, why are you doing this to me?! An immense pain floods my entire being. The pain of despair. *Of completely fucking this up.*

I'll win.

I'll win.

Won't I?

Don't panic.

DON'T panic.

Panicking, I pick up the phone. I dial iTrade and am put on hold. *Come on!* A live voice finally comes on the line, "iTrade, how can I help you?"

"I'm holding 9,877 shares of BBBY! The stock's getting hammered! Earnings came out this morning and they were supposed to be good! I don't understand how this is going down—"

"Account number please."

I try to concentrate, try to remain calm.

I get up and start pacing, spitting out my account number. "I need more margin money! NOW!"

The live voice says: "Ms. Marco, your pro-day trading status allowed you to purchase $857,000 on margin. You don't have any more buying power left. Your balance is negative $152,390. The trade went against you. I'm sorry, but you need to wire more money into your account or sell out of your position."

My heart pounds. Everything registers. It's like the very ground is going out from under me.

I have no money left to wire in.

I want to scream. *Or run.* Slowly, as if in a nightmare, I click the mouse, sell the shares, and take the loss.

A message comes across my screen: SOLD 8500 BBBY shares = Gains/"LOSSES" FLASH in RED —$385,626.

I put my hands over my mouth:"Nooooooooooooooooooooo!"

The scream is in full agony and desolation, as broken and forsaken as the wail of a lost child.

* * *

I blindly make my way into the bathroom. Holding onto the walls to steady myself, I turn on the light and recoil from the brightness.

Grabbing the edges of the sink, I slowly open my eyes. Shattered, I stare at myself in the mirror.

Retirement...gone.

Savings...decimated.

Trust...violated...

I'm unaware of the hour, abandoned in my misery, and my eyes blaze with delirium.

I open the medicine cabinet and stare at five bottles of pills. My cat nudges at my legs meowing. I pull down one of the pill bottles, open it, and stare into the bottle.

In the darkest darkness.

* * *

Rain comes down in lashing torrents. I stand at my father's houseboat and knock on his door. My face is wet with water and the rain is so heavy, it feels like a relentless waterfall.

I look through the window and see my father is asleep in his chair. His eyes are closed and there's no life in his face.

I stand there, drenched and dripping. Every bone in my body aches and I'm weighed down by shock.

I knock again and my father awakens and comes to the window. When he sees me standing there, his face positively lights up.

He opens the door, "What happened?"

I walk in. My father sits back down in his chair, as the rain pounds at the ceiling.

His vivid eyes concentrate on mine. I begin hesitantly, choking back tears, my hands twitching, my sentences disjointed. "I was at swim practice…I checked the price…I took a big position… it gapped down…when I got home … I got …a margin call… Oh, Dad."

I can barely look at him. I'm seized with shame and my heart aches with the most genuine sorrow.

"When did this happen?"

"…Few hours ago."

My head hurts, my eyes hurt, my stomach hurts. It hurts and I deserve it.

"I did everything I could, Dad… I never thought… anything like this… I tried to…"

He holds up his hand to cease my incoherent flow of words. Innumerable questions must run through his mind but he reserves them all for later.

"How much is lost?" he asks.

"Almost all of it." I drop my eyes, not elucidating further.

"Almost all of it?" he repeats, incredulous.

He sits perfectly rigid in his chair and his face is an unreadable mask. He remains so still he may have turned to stone.

It's an irrevocable mistake, he must realize. *To give me this money.*

"They missed on revenues by .48 cents. Third quarter EPS guided down below consensus, their second quarter comps were down 1%…"

I lay the file down on the table and he looks at it lying there like a coiled and venomous snake. His eyes do not leave it; it's proof of his financial ruin.

"I'm surprised you didn't send Troy over to tell me," he says, "That impresses me." And then he turns away, "Not that I'm not screwed."

He stands up and walks over to the window. The rain runs in rivulets down the glass of the window like his money that has just been poured down the rat hole.

It's as if our whole world stops.

"I am so sorry, Dad." My eyes are lost and empty, my voice, leaden with sorrow.

His concentration broken, he looks back at me, and I summon every last ounce of energy. "I swear to you, Dad, everything I'm going to do is to earn that money back. Do you hear me?"

I take steely control of myself and rise, facing my father. "Every penny I lost — I'm going to earn it all back for you, Dad, I promise—"

My father raises an eyebrow, doubtful.

5

Chapter 5

It's a grey day. Brittany and I jog down Marina Boulevard.

"It's game over, huh? Isn't that how Troy blew up? On margin?"

I keep running and don't say anything. I'm at a complete loss for words.

"Jolette, should I feel guilty? It was my idea to help your father with his money..."

"No. Not your fault. Nobody knew Blood Bath and Beyond would tank like that. I landed a job. It's all going to work out." I pick up speed, trying to hold it together with a distant resolve.

"Did you? Doing what?" Brittany asks. "You know your history with jobs has never been good."

"I'm an assistant. On a trading floor. Like I said, it's all going to work out."

I keep running, trying to forget everything, trying to forget that I'm even alive.

* * *

"The total market capitalization of the U.S. stock market is $48 trillion dollars..."

In expensive underwear and bra, I roll on nylons, remembering the job interview. "And as they say, in all financial markets, past performance is never a guarantee of the future."

Getting ready for work, I watch CNBC market news.

"Assistants come and go but there's one open position working for Monique Levine, Senior Vice President, in our institutional equity sales department..."

I slip my feet into black high heels, watching the clock ... 4:03 a.m.

"She trades large blocks of stocks on behalf of Wall Street institutions, or better known as hedge funds..."

I have my morning routine down to a science; feed Sam, followed by two minutes in the shower, and then I hold the blow dryer to my head in a trancelike manner. Streaking on Chanel's dark green eyeliner and crème colored eye shadow, I brush Christian Dior mascara onto my long lashes.

"And as an Assistant, you'll be paid forty thousand dollars a year to start."

Inspecting several designer suits hanging neatly in the closet, I choose one. Fully dressed and standing in front of a mirror, I examine myself. I lost six pounds since I've started this job.

Stress.

"When Monique says jump, you ask how high..."

I move toward my computer. It's covered with a POISON SIGN and the words: "NO TRADING."

Beside it is a NOTEBOOK. On Page 1, there's a PAYMENT PLAN: EARNED + $3800. NOW NEED: = $281,826.

Underneath it is a list of GENERAL RESOLVES:

1. No Starbucks
2. No new shoes.

3. No movies.
4. No buying books. Library ONLY.
5. Only spend $15.00 — (crossed out) — $10.00 a week for myself.
6. Be nicer to Troy and Sarah — (crossed out) — IGNORE TROY AND SARAH UNTIL I EARN THIS MONEY BACK.
7. Cancel triathlon with Brittany.

I close the notebook.

Sacrifice.

I will make tremendous sacrifices until I earn this money back. I look at the clock again: 4:12 a.m.

Time to go!

I turn off the light, and quietly close my door so I don't wake up my neighbors. Rushing down the four flights of stairs to my building lobby in the heart of the marina district in San Francisco, I pick up a WALL STREET JOURNAL that's lying on the lobby floor, and gaze over the headlines. *What is the market going to do today?*

Pacing back and forth, I wait for my ride to arrive. It's pitch dark outside and eerily quiet. I always wait inside and try to busy myself with the newspaper, too afraid to learn what's lurking around outdoors.

My carpool arrives on time, and when I see the Lexus' headlights' play through the fog, I come outside.

The three traders swerve and miss running me over by mere inches. They engage in this ritual every morning and think it's hysterical.

One day they will finally hit me, I think... but that wouldn't be as bad as being late because once those doors close to that research meeting at exactly 4:45 a.m. and not a second later, you weren't allowed inside. And if Monique doesn't get her morning notes... *you'd wish you were dead.*

"What did you do last night, Jolette?" Nicholas, the driver, asks. He's a blue blooded options trader with a dry wit and large appetite for partying. His bloodshot eyes peer through me from the rear view mirror.

"Yeah, Jolette," Joshua echoes, an egomaniac with an unbeatable body. His dark hair is still dripping wet. "Another hot date with your boyfriend?"

Date.

Right.

I ignore their questions and stare out the window, looking into darkness. I admire the Golden Gate Bridge lit up like a string of diamonds. A stream of thick fog snakes and wraps its way around Pacific Heights.

"Come on, Jolette, you're so hot, tell us what's up," Nicholas pleads.

They drill me every day this way. Each day it's the same questions. And each day, I ignore them… like strangers in the airport.

Finally, we pull into the parking lot. Nicholas grabs the parking ticket, I jump out at the gate.

The traders can listen to the meeting at their desks, but I'm in sales and I have to be in the meeting; present, awake, and *ready to roll.*

* * *

Entering 555 California Street, I flash my security card and jam into the packed elevators. Our building holds all the top brokerage houses on the street: Merrill, Goldman, J.P. Morgan, Morgan Stanley. And inside, it's alive. It always is, even at this hour.

I'm aware of how the talking amongst the men would come to a stop as I enter the elevator. Maybe they didn't want me to hear their conversation: stocks, sports, girls, lewd jokes; who knew?

Does it matter? I look at my watch.

Come on. Come on!

4:44...Let's go...

The doors to the 36th floor open. The trading floor. Three quarters of the elevator piles out, most carrying coffee, others too early to fathom it. All pick up their newspapers of choice on the floor: The Wall Street Journal, Daily Deal, Investor's Business Daily.

Doors shut.

Reopen on 37.

I exit first, one of the benefits of being a female, and slide my security card through. I wait for the light to turn green, every second counts, and open the heavy door.

I walk down the long hallway, hampered by my high heels and briefcase, and now I'm running... *Fifteen seconds!*

I enter the meeting with the other brokers, investment bankers, and analysts. I try not to let it show that I almost didn't make it on time, and if you aren't awake by now, you never will be.

We pick up the research reports lying along the far side of the room and take a seat. The meeting is not set up auditorium style like other brokerage houses. The most prominent analysts and managing directors sit at a head table in the center of the room, and everyone else scatters to find chairs around them. The lower down the totem pole you are, the further away from that head table you sat. I'm almost all the way in the back.

Six clocks display time zones in London, Paris, Chicago, Boston, New York, and San Francisco. Analysts are teleconferenced in from the other offices over satellite TV's. It's one big production. The blinds are closed not to remind us that the rest of the world is at home, still sleeping.

And we are not.

We are here because we work at ABLX Securities.

And we move the global financial markets...

The austere vibe that hangs in the air signifies this is a place of vast wealth; a firm of blue blooded individuals who come from good families and have top-notched educations.

I did not come from an Ivy League background; Monique Levine needed an assistant and I landed the interview and scored the job. I became licensed Series 7 & 63, and when Monique learned of my multi-tasking capabilities and inherent trading abilities, I was thrown into the trenches.

"Let's go everyone!"

An investment banker starts to speak magisterially, basking in the glory of his latest deal. Ninety brokers and analysts sit hypnotized to the information being revealed.

Next up is banking analyst, Paul Zucker. He rises and moves to the podium. Navy blue suspenders divide his starched white shirt and brightly colored Ferragamo tie which falls smartly from his neck.

"Good morning, everyone. Siemens, Germany's largest bank, estimated it made $60.7 billion in the fourth quarter as the global rebound increased its bottom line."

He eyes me. I look up and catch his look, then turn away, jotting down notes.

I remember researching this bank six months ago. It had plenty of operation expenses and revenues were falling quarter over quarter and now *he's upgrading it?* It didn't make sense. *Something was off.*

Paul and I used to date. We met at a Halloween party in Pacific Heights and he was dressed as a bum. He kept saying, "Transformation is possible." The last time we saw each other, he came over to my apartment because he needed to use my landline. I didn't want him in my apartment, so I let him use my phone out in the hallway.

I was working full time from home and I was day trading. I was trapped in a trade, waiting. Bored, I brought Paul some water in the hallway, and as I stood over him, I watched him.

He sat in the small, wooden chair with his head leaned against the wall. He looked worn out and tired, like his job was beginning to take its toll on him. Maybe he was losing control, the same way I had lost control many times trading.

But he sat confidently, with two legs on the ground, undeterred. He continued his phone conversation as if I wasn't even there. He looked sexy. I could tell so much about a man by the way they sat and the way they walked. I was a master observer of human behavior. People behaved like stocks with predictable reactions, patterns, and fluctuations. Paul, with his legs spread apart and his eyes looking up at me, looked strong and weak at the same time. I brushed my hand over his thigh.

He grabbed my hand and put it over his crotch. He was hard. I could hear the other guy yelling through the phone; margins and revenues were being discussed and argued about over and over again. Paul ran his hand through his hair exasperated. I climbed on top of him, and rubbed myself against him, leaning down, whispering in his ear, "Does this feel good?" I kept going despite the fact that he was ignoring me, "Does it, Paul?"

He leaned further down in the chair so I could keep going, giving me more space.

"I understand," Paul concluded, closing his eyes, as I moved up and down on him, watching his eyes roll back in his head.

I took the phone from him when his conversation ended, and let it drop to the ground.

"Paul, can we do this here?"

"Now?"

"Yes." I unzipped his pants and at the same time, slipped out of my shorts. I sat down on him again and with experienced fingers, lifted him inside of me, playing with him, teasing him, and Paul, going with it, pressed me down on him harder, grabbing me by the waist, "Ride my cock, I want you to come all over me."

I smiled inwardly. I controlled the pace, the angle, and once I leaned forward and pressed myself against him in that certain spot, it would be all over. I wanted it to last, I tried to wait…it felt so good….

Then DING went the elevator bell, and in seconds those doors would open, and somebody would be coming down the hall.

Instead of stopping, I kept going, faster, picking up the pace, squeezing him harder beneath me whispering Paul, Paul Paullllllllll and then those fire doors opened and this girl was coming down the hall, and I, mid orgasm, let out a groan and collapsed into Paul, and Paul, stunned and spent, looked back at the girl, then me, like a deer in the headlights.

He's called me numerous times since and now that I'm working here, it's worse.

The meeting drones on and on and I just wish I was at home trading.

Phillip Peters, the stern "in the know," Managing Director, eyes everyone in the room, "That's it, everyone! Go to work!"

I rise with the other stockbrokers and analysts and stampede out the door.

Paul follows, "Hey Jolette, how's it going? I saw Monique down in the compliance office this morning. She's on the war path again. She still livin' the Benson account?"

"…Wouldn't you be?"

Jamming into the stairwell with the other brokers, I rush up the stairs, leaving Paul in the dust.

6

Chapter 6

My high heels click against the marble floor and it sounds like a ticking time bomb… TICK. TICK. TICK. I keep moving toward those large double doors, the doors swing open, and the morning bell sounds –

Rows and rows of hundreds of brokers shout behind the newest flat panel screens, punching keyboards, yelling out orders!

"Big seller in Qualcomm!… Dump it! 250,000 at a half? What are you, pregnant?! You don't want to marry the stock! Short five hundred thousand…"

I thread my way across the massive trading floor. Traders glance up as I pass.

Arriving to my desk, I throw my briefcase down, put my headset on, and pick up a ringing line. "Trading!"

"Jolette, is that you? I need to liquidate my UBER shares. The stock's climbing, how much am I holding?"

"We need to GET OUT!" my boss, Monique, orders. "SELL IT ALL! What part of sell don't you fucking understand?!" I sit right beside her on the trading floor, and she manages clients who have over two trillion dollars in assets.

Most of her business comes from the almighty Benson account: Steve Benson, the biggest hedge fund manager on Wall Street.

Monique looks up and our eyes meet. She has fine aristocratic features, ruby-red lips, blonde hair, and she's always beautifully groomed. I point to the pile of research reports I put on her desk.

She covers the mouthpiece, "What did Zucker come out with?"

"Siemens – long."

I turn my attention back to the client on the phone, "For which account, Richard?"

Monique continues, "Benson generates ninety million a quarter and I will not lose another account to Rothman!" she yells into the phone.

"I don't know!" Richard snaps back. "Check the CGC Limited Partnership."

Richard is a top tiered Silicon Valley venture capitalist and he believes that I and everybody else on Monique's team should know his holdings by heart. But he doesn't realize that we have 100's of other Richards with 100's of other accounts, and we're so busy we can't keep it all straight.

The markets hitting all time highs doesn't help this.

Doesn't help it at all.

I hit up Richard's account on my screen and peruse his holdings. My eyes dart from screen to screen like a marble in a pinball machine. I have seven large 16" inch screens piled on top of each other.

For a moment, I forget all the money that I'm losing in Bed, Bath, and Beyond.

For another moment, I don't worry if my paycheck will hit my checking account Friday before my rent payment gets deducted from it.

And for another moment, I don't ask myself the million dollar question: *How will I ever get ahead in life?*

"You have 534,000 shares, Richard, but the shares are restricted. You can't sell until the lock-up period expires."

I hear Monique's voice again. "What is he doing, Jolette?! Does he want to sell? I don't want any mistakes! I'm going to have a heart attack!"

"Richard, let me run this by Monique, okay? I'll see what we can do."

"Tell her I want in on the Lever IPO this Thursday! You guys stiffed me on the last deal!"

I stare at the astronomical amount of shares that he holds in his account already: 1,213,444 AMZN, 2,589,988 TSLA, 5,201,000 AAPL, 4,200,000 TLR... the list goes on and on.

And he just wants ... *more.*

I hang up and Monique is hanging over my shoulder.

"We haven't cleaned the stock yet on the UBER shares," I tell her before she has a chance to blow a gasket.

"Why not?!" she sneers. "You worked all weekend, why wasn't this taken care of?"

"The attorneys don't respond to emails on the weekends, I've already told you that." A thousand times, I want to add, but I can't afford to piss her off with a bad tone.

She gives me a discerning look. "Kimberly, get over here!"

Her young waif of an assistant, the one who has worked for her for the past two years but probably makes five times as much as I do, sashays over. "Yes, Monique?"

"What can we do about the UBER distribution? Can you talk to the transfer agency?! How can we speed along this process?! Damn it!"

Kimberly hovers over me, hitting some keys on my keyboard, and I feel her breath on my neck. Between her and Monique so close to me, I feel like I'm suffocating.

"The lockup period expires Friday. If we sell him out today, we can cancel and rebook the trade, and then finish the paperwork. We'll use a trade date of Friday..."

There we go, Kimberly, nice work, more ways to milk the system...As the rich get richer...

"Do it," Monique snaps.

Somebody yells, "I've got Benson line three!" All heads look up as the word "Benson."

"I've got it!" Monique shouts, and sits back down in her chair.

Another line rings, I grab it. "Trading!"

The minutes slip into hours. The phones never stop ringing. At noon, Monique says, "Jolette, go down to Jamba and get us some smoothies!"

"Yes, Monique."

I reach for a twenty in my briefcase and take off. Stopping by Kimberly's desk, I ask her and Robbie Firestone, another one of Monique's assistants, if they want anything. They both shake their heads, no, and go back to their calls.

I have seven minutes to get the smoothies and run right back. *Seven minutes of glory to get away from the trading desk.*

I look at my watch and it's already peak lunch hour and I know I'll be standing in a long line as Monique fumes back at her desk wondering what's taking so long.

Leaving the building, I catch my first glimpse of daylight. The sky is fantastic: bright blue and not a cloud in the sky. The noise coming from the traffic momentarily drowns out the screaming from the trading desk, and as I walk the short block to Jamba Juice, I inhale the cool San Francisco air.

Heaven.

"Good morning," I say to the girls at the counter.

"Hey, Jolette! How are you today?"

"Good, thank you."

Invariably pressed for time, I quickly order. "Two orange smoothies and these pretzels, please."

My hand trembles from low blood sugar as I hand them my money.

"Coming right up!" they say with a smile. I'm grateful for their kindness and see them everyday around the same time. My voice is usually unsteady from the stress. I stick a five dollar bill in their tip jar, and move aside so the others can order.

Devouring the pretzels, I lean back against the wall and struggle to catch my breath. Working late for Monique again last night, I passed out into oblivion without any dinner.

I take out my phone and check BBBY. I still have a few shares left, but it's nothing to get rich off of, and it's still down anyway. It breaks my heart and I'd give anything to undo that trade.

Every trader should get one redo, I think. One trade that you can just give back.

BBBY... the light of my life, juices of my core, an unyielding yearning, my sin, my error... You are more of a trip than freebasing crack...You are just ... heart wrenching.

Another grave mistake.

It's been two months since I've placed a trade and I feel dead without it. I'm trapped in this ABLX job and this fledging BBBY position. Going into work every day feels like a time bomb ready to explode. I'm ignored, ridiculed and badgered all day long. "Do this, Jolette! Hurry up, Jolette! Get it right, Jolette! Not again, Jolette! Come on, Jolette! What the fuck, Jolette?!"

Even in my sleep, I hear Monique's voice.

But I have no other option but to survive this.

And *I will.*

I will get out of this hole, I tell myself.

When I look up, something catches my eye. I see a woman who looks like my mother and she bends down and says something to a young girl. The girl is crying and the woman bends down and hugs her. "It'll be okay, sweetie, it'll be okay."

As I watch this, I'm touched. My mother never hugged me this way, and I was never allowed to cry.

The young girl says ... "I wish... I wish..." I can't hear the rest of her sentence but suddenly I hear my own mother's voice: "I wish you were never born."

* * *

I get off the elevator carrying the smoothies, walking past the other stockbrokers in the retail group. They're the ones who aren't screaming. They have their lunches spread out and they're calmly watching the tape. I overhear one of them laughing on the phone, "And get waxed, Tina, I don't like razor stubble on my tongue."

As I get closer to the Institutional Sales department, I can feel the pressure mounting. I hear Monique and the other brokers yelling from ten rows back. The phones are still ringing, and the chaos is still alive and going strong.

I drop the smoothie on Monique's desk. "Preston's on hold. Infinity just went public! Pick him up!"

"Which line?"

"Line ten. Hurry up!"

I find line ten on the massive turret phone and answer it. Sticking my straw in the smoothie, I look up at the clock: 12:20 p.m.

Forty minutes until the market closes.

Forty and counting.

* * *

At 1:00 p.m., the market closes, and Monique's group of about thirteen young stockbroker trainees, mostly men, rise from their desks, mixing and talking. I smile at Kimberly as we remove our headsets.

Monique nods in my direction. "Jolette, walk with me down to the cage. I want to talk to you."

I get up. Nobody likes going down to the cage. It's where the Operations team sits and they deal with problems like trading errors or problem account paperwork.

We cross the trading floor. "The numbers show you're doing well," she begins, "Top five percent of your class. But you're continually tardy…"

A group of male brokers pass us joking around. "What? I'm never late," I respond.

She cuts me off. "An assignment's come up and I thought about you. Not really a job, more of a – *favor*. You know the MEDCO launch is tonight. We're one of the lead bankers and it's —"

"—Slated to be the biggest deal of the quarter."

"Well, yes, though they say that about every deal. I'm trying to get my hands on our competitors who are after the Benson account. They have a tendency to brag, these guys, and you know how to talk to them, don't you?"

I nod, not sure where this is going.

"You see, the one I want to know about, won't speak to me, and I want you to go after him tonight at the launch party."

"Who?"

"Rothman Institutional broker, Noel Sheffield."

I stop walking and go very still. "The master of the market — ?"

Monique turns and faces me. She doesn't say anything, just examines my face.

"I appreciate the opportunity, Monique, but… why me?"

"You're always late, you owe me. Plus, you're determined and available and I can't spare another trainee right now. Most are studying for their Series 7 exams and you've already passed yours."

Monique turns and begins to walk at a faster clip. I rush to keep up.

"I doubt that he'll speak to you, but I want you to say you tried. He's a clever broker, and he knows… everything."

Monique hands me a folder. "Here's the 411 on him, hedge funds he covers, a special pass for you to get in to the event tonight. If he won't talk, I want to know who he's talking to. I want to hear everything and – keep this quiet."

We reach the cage and Jesus Menendez, an under-dressed young man sitting behind bars, reaches for the documents Monique hands him. "More Benson accounts, Hey-Zeus, did you send those wires?"

She smiles. Satan's smile. Jesus nods, jittery. He takes the files Monique hands him, and we walk off.

She puts her hand on my shoulder. "Now I want you to make this a priority, okay?"

I nod, hesitant.

"Robbie will point out who he is. Be really cautious with Noel Sheffield. Don't notify him of anything private, Jolette, and trust me on this, you don't want Noel Sheffield inside in your pants. Just do me this favor, but never disregard what he is…"

"What's that, Monique?" I ask, unnerved.

"A player. A total narcissist…"

7

Chapter 7

A line of limousines snake their way toward the entrance. Streets are blocked off. The Investment Banking Event is packed and overflowing with people. Illuminated fountains spell out M E D C O in cascades of water.

I step off the bus.

The venue at Pier 53 has been transformed into a Swiss Castle. Sumptuous. Magnificent by any standards. A five million price tag for the world's elite where no expense is spared.

I move toward the entrance and approach the long check-in line. Loud music, voices, laughter all become audible.

Clutching my ID in hand, I look down at my photo with the official looking ABLX Securities logo. It names me 'Vice President, Trading.' A security guard eyes me up and down, clicks his wand over my badge, and as I hold in my breath, he says, "Enjoy."

I glide inside the ethereal tent, relieved. There's a little thrill I get at doing this; at getting into this event that I'm not really supposed to be at.

Looking around, movers and shakers mix with Cirque de Soleil performers, circus animals, and scantily clad women.

A band plays in every corner. There are fire eaters. A white tiger. Open bars. I marvel at the atmosphere. Every delicacy of food is offered. There are massive seafood tables with oysters, gulf shrimp and lobster tails. They have baby back ribs with lime jelly, sushi, Chinese dumplings, all kinds of gourmet pizzas, caviar stations, everything you can imagine – *it's here.*

I take a plate and enjoy some shrimp and steak skewers and Robbie finds me within five minutes. "I've been waiting for you, Jolette, let's go."

I leave my plate behind on a table and follow him. We move through the press of bodies. "Noel Sheffield is our greatest threat. Covers every major hedge fund on Wall Street," he says, as we pass a man on stilts. "We get a lot of brokers going to these events, but I can't remember seeing one so… hot…"

He turns back to me. "Will you be staying late tonight? Because these events can be quite a lot of… fun."

I have no intentions of staying after I meet Noel Sheffield, and I am able to bring something, *any type of information,* back to Monique.

The truth of it is, no matter how grand this thing is, I'd still rather be at home with my cat, studying stock charts.

"Robbie, we have that 4:45 a.m. research meeting tomorrow," I remind him, my excuse as always.

"That's right. Let's make this fast then, I have my own accounts to talk to."

We enter a stairwell and a bulky iron gate clangs shut behind us. We reach the top floor and Robbie steers me over to the balcony, and we overlook the crowd.

"Sheffield's at the very top of the Wall Street pyramid. You know the culture; the more important you are, the less you need to be seen, but he should be here."

And then Robbie spots him. "There he is. 10 o'clock. Navy blue suit.

He's reading his cell phone standing with, I think that's Guy Usami..."

I look over and see him.

Noel Sheffield.

He's standing with a group of men, the drink in his hand is untouched, and the look on his face is serious. I watch as he surveys the room like a veteran. He's a man in control — a man who works hard and will not stop until he reaches the top. He has an air of power about him.

But there's something else about Noel. A vulnerability. I can sense it from all the way up here. A secret, perhaps. A void.

I'm about to say something to Robbie, lost in my thoughts, swallowed up in lust in one second, but when I turn, Robbie is no longer there.

* * *

Time has elapsed. Groups have changed. Voices are louder. The San Francisco Investment Banking event is in full swing. I walk around, following Noel, tracking his every move.

He's now holding court with a different group of hedge fund managers; they're all of the same ilk; expensive suits, ivy league mannerisms.

I watch him over the rim of my Chardonnay glass. I'm standing with a small group of Monique's high net worth clients listening to a smug healthcare CEO explain the world.

"You want economic truth, you need to hit the small investor. You don't jeopardize our financial markets by some hypocritical stance on drug consumption."

A Money Manager remarks, "I've just seen a troubling report on the company. According to these numbers, their credit ratings could fall to junk status."

"Sounds like someone's planting dark Intel," the CEO says, chuckling,

"Hey, not us…"

At first, I was apprehensive about attending this event, but after I began to unwind in this surreal atmosphere, I was able to enjoy myself. Maybe I have a future at ABLX, I start to think, as I watch Noel Sheffield once more.

I'm arrested by his handsome face and sensual mouth. He looks distinguished and powerful, and by the way he carries himself, he's extremely proud of his achievements and stance on Wall Street.

He's now standing with Paul Zucker, and Paul points to me and says something to him. When Noel sees me looking at him, his eyes bear into mine.

A ripple of excitement floods through me. I feel confident, strong. It's a confidence I don't deserve but I'm enjoying this little game nonetheless. I mean, after all, Monique put me up to this. I would never be here on my own, chasing him.

No, of course not.

This is business.

And I intended to keep it that way.

I excuse myself and move closer to him. Men stop talking and look up as I pass. Striding with a newfound purpose, I turn and look at Noel once more. I definitely have his attention now.

Our eyes lock.

I take a glass of Perrier from a waiter and move on, but then I look back … *just once.*

And it says... everything.

* * *

Standing outside on the balcony, I lean up against the railing. The cool breeze touches my cheeks, and I stare out onto the water. When I look down, the most expensive pair of brown leather loafers that I have ever seen in my life appear beside me.

I don't even have to turn. I already know who it is.

Noel Sheffield.

We stare out onto the glittering harbor together. I can feel the warmth of his body, and we're locked in a prolonged moment of silence.

I learned long ago that silence is a powerful instrument. People are usually uncomfortable in it and seek to fill it, revealing much in the process. So I play my card …and wait.

"You see that yacht over there?" he says. "Someday… mine's gonna be bigger."

I can't help but smile. "Size matters."

"My priority is your satisfaction," he replies, with an edge to his voice.

Great comeback. Great. I'm turned on. And intrigued. I turn to him, "I bet you have a lot of priorities."

"I bet you're right. Are you a betting woman?" he asks. His eyes bear into mine and a bolt of electricity charges through me.

No one should look into those blue eyes. Ever. They rake into my soul. And his question cuts right through me. "No," I reply, mechanically.

"Good. I'm Noel. Noel Sheffield, Rothman." He holds an outstretched hand.

I hesitate. I don't want to touch him. I'm afraid of what it'll do to me. But slowly, tentatively, my fingertips touch his. I feel the softness of his hand, and when I let go, Noel tightens his grip like a vice. "Nice to meet you."

A fireworks and laser show begins in the sky, and Jason Stein approaches us. He runs a large hedge fund and I spent the earlier part of the evening speaking to him. Noel gestures a greeting, but he's not coming to talk to Noel.

"Jolette, I'll look into those names you mentioned, and we'll open a new account tomorrow. I'll let Monique know as well."

I nod and he strolls off to join another well-known hedge fund manager holding court across the room.

"You work with Monique Levine," Noel states, eyeing me.

I nod.

"We're rivals. You cover the Benson account."

"You know your competition."

"You'd be surprised at how much I know..."

"So surprise me," I push.

He gazes up at the twilight sky with a look of contentment. "I love this freezing cold city. The Silicon Valley, the deals, the launches, the big score. You know the best thing about Wall Street of the West is everything you can do here. And the worst is... everything you can't."

He runs his fingers through his hair distractedly. "You want to make some serious money? Take a look at Stellar. It's in beast mode. They're going to create an entire smart economy – it's the future of blockchain."

"Trading that space is like walking outside in a thunderstorm holding a metal rod."

"Not true. They're releasing a new integrated processor. Word isn't out yet. They'll become real players when their transactions settle in two to five seconds, allowing users to exchange government-backed currencies like U.S. dollars to euros."

My thoughts start racing. "That's interesting. Where did you hear this?"

"I'm in the flow of information. I don't predict the market, I create it."

His voice is soothing, articulate, and dangerously comforting.

"All of life is a game of luck."

"A real man makes his own luck. Benson holds it in his portfolio. Might not be a bad time for him to pick up more..."

"I don't have access to Benson," I reply evenly. "What other companies do you like?"

Jason Stein is angling for me to join him across the balcony, but I'm too focused on Noel.

Noel reads something on his cell phone, and then he looks back at me. "I have some clients to talk to, but we should meet again."

It's a dismissal. And I don't like it.

"You ever get time for a drink?" he asks.

"Not really. Maybe someday."

"Well, I'll call you. Meanwhile, keep your eye on Stellar. You tell me if that's luck."

He turns, and walks away with a look that would turn anyone to stone.

I stand there, blown away.

8

Chapter 8

In the cab on my way home, I check my cell phone, and my brother has called six times. I call him right back. "Everything okay, Troy?"

"No. What happened to Dad's money, Jolette? You buried him, didn't you?"

Not the greeting I was hoping for.

"Troy, I have everything under control."

"You have nothing under control. In fact, you are completely out of control."

I try to focus on which way this cab driver is going so I won't have to pay bank for this ride because I only have a twenty dollar bill in my wallet, and my brother keeps harping on me, "Jolette, try Gamblers Anonymous, it's helped a lot of people."

"Troy, I feel really bad, but I'm working now, and I'm going to take care of everything."

"You remember what happened to me...You remember how that overly manipulated stock market took my money. ALLOFFFITTT," he slurs. "You worked with me, you were therrrrre... We were short. Jerome Powell is the crook of all crooks, a master manipulator...

rigging this market to the upside…"

I can tell Troy has been drinking again. "We the people have no control over anything in our lives. The elite control it all. They keep us down. They take our rights away. They do not want us to succeed in any way. Our government and the elite want to control it all. They tell us what they want us to hear. They feed fear and the people believe. Whyyyyy? Why do we believe because we have become programmed to their ways. We are not free. We will never be free from debt. From our jobs. Free to do what we want. We, as Americans, live in the freest country in the world, but I feel liked I'm locked up in Alcatraz, Jolette…Everyday….ALCATRAZ…"

"Stop complaining, Troy, and do something about it. How's your delivery job going?"

"I quit," he stammers.

"You quit?"

"Yeah. You know how many rides I had to make just to get paid minimum wage? How about all the pressure I was under? They don't care about their employees! It's all about the stock price and the shareholders. They cut your benefits down to nothing, work you to the bone, and pay you jack shit. I'm making more on unemployment."

"Okay, Troy, it's late, just hang in there. Things will get better," I conclude as the cab pulls up to my apartment. "I have a plan and everything's going to work out. Bye."

"Another plan…?!" he splutters, "What's your plan now?!" but I hit end call.

* * *

As soon as I get inside, I get on the phone with the banks. Credit card cash advances. That's what I needed. And I needed them now. If Noel is right about Stellar, then this could be it.

This could be the quick fix that I need not only recoup my money back, but to stop having to go into work at 4:00 in the morning, not to mention – working *weekends.* I wanted my life back.

I wanted my freedom. In a way, my brother is right. Wall Street beat me up. And my brother. And my father.

It's time to regain control.

By 11:00 p.m., my three bank loans go off without a hitch, one of the benefits of having a job, and I'm allotted $10,000 from each of my three credit cards. The money will roll over tomorrow to my checking, and from my checking, I'll transfer it over to iTrade.

Then I'll start again.

I'll start trading.

A shot of elation goes through me and I feel like I've come alive for the first time in weeks.

I'm suddenly filled with one of life's most desirous feeling: *hope.* For when that is taken away, a person is left with nothing.

I gaze over my hammered portfolio and see that I'm still down 75%. It's not just the money that's lost that's the travesty, but *the hope.* The lost hope of all the things that I was going to do with that money…

I look at the Bed Bath and Beyond chart like I would a lost lover. I watch it from work, every day, all day. "Every move you make, every dip you take, every pump you fake, every support you break… I'll be watching you…" I hum, as I pet my cat. "We're going to be okay, Sammy! Stick with me and I will lead you to the promised land!"

I make my way for the shower and when I get out, I'm too jacked up to sleep.

I flop on my bed with my pink blanket, my iPad, and begin to study the stock chart of Stellar with ferocious intensity.

My cell phone rings: *Monique.*

"Well?" she asks.

"I emailed you everything. Right down to the brand of shoes he was wearing."

"You didn't leave anything out?"

"No."

"He didn't mention any stocks he was trading?"

"I told you blockchain and the miners, in general. Mentioned Stellar, but..."

"It's a Sienna knockoff. Short interest is too high."

"They just announced a partnership with United to develop a cross border payment system. Resistance is tracking about eighty dollars, the above trend line of a descending channel..."

My cat is purring beside me, but I sense alarm on the other end of the line. "What's wrong, Monique?"

"Benson threatened to move the account."

"What? Where?"

"There's been some problems booking the trades. They're trying to blame it on you. I informed them that your work is impeccable —"

I go silent.

"Jolette?"

"Yeah, I'm here, Monique. I just don't know what to say, I mean..."

"I'll cover for you, Jolette, don't worry. You won't lose your job. But keep a close watch on Noel, will you?"

"Mommy, Mommy, my head hurts," I hear in the background. Word is among the other associates that Monique has a special needs child at home.

"Okay, sweetie, I'll be with you in just a moment," Monique says, and then she turns her attention back on me. "I need you to run with this, okay?"

She clicks off, leaving me sitting there, alarmed at the tone in her voice.

I pull up my iTrade account and stare – escaping into the numbers.

9

Chapter 9

When my alarm goes off the next morning, I'm eager to be up and on my way.

My cat gets an earful of excited chatter as I rush through my morning routine. "Maybe I'll give Jason Stein the tip and he'll pay us with commission business. Those commissions for Monique will ensure that I get a good year end bonus…"

My cat watches me with yellow eyes that are as big and lovely as great jewels, and I grin as I share with him my plan.

"So many different accounts, Sammy my sweet. … You get the idea. There'll be a diamond collar in it for you in the end, and before you know it, we'll be back to day trading too!" I croon, giving my treasured furball an extra squeeze before sailing out the door.

"Hey guys!" I greet my carpoolers minutes later, sounding so unlike my usual self.

The traders turn in unison to gape.

"Out with it, Jolette," Nicholas demands, "It's criminal to keep sex that great to yourself."

"Whatever do you mean?" I respond with an exaggerated movie-starish bat of my lush lashes.

"Oh, come on, Jolette. From the way you look this morning, that guy must be one great batter, a homerun king. You've got Drew here thinkin' bout changing teams," Joshua chides.

This brings predictable howls of protests from the others, but as usual, I ignore them.

Not being able to pry a single detail about my evening, the traders spend the rest of the ride discussing business.

"Are you still trading for Albertson Capital, Josh?"

"Yeah, they made a *killing* yesterday. Close to fifty million on that Infinity IPO. And it's not over."

"His partner just bought the Moller M400 Skycar. A flying car!"

"So Benson just bought his own island…"

"What's that like, Jolette, being on the team that covers Benson?" Nicholas asks. "Have you talked to him yet?"

"No, Monique won't allow it."

"I'd give anything to work for him," Drew admits.

Me too, I think again.

Benson LLC – A club everybody wanted to get into – and even the best sometimes didn't qualify.

I check my watch again.

For now, I work at ABLX Securities.

So let's go!

Drive, Nicholas! Drive!

* * *

Passing Robbie Firestone as I take my seat on the trading floor, I notice a prominent cut slashed across his forehead. "Hey Robbie, how's the slaughterer?"

"Let me know what they released in research and I'll tell ya."

I pull out my stack of research reports. "Jansen upgraded Tenet but

I'd go long Stellar," I say mischievously.

"Stellar?"

"That's right. *Stellar.* What happened to you?" I ask, pointing to his head.

"Oh just walked into a wall last night after the party. Where did you go? I was looking for you."

"I was there. Stayed late, had a blast," I exaggerate.

Monique eyes me as I sit down and moments later, the morning bell sounds. Like birds fluttering in sudden flight, we all whirl around to go to work! They're *off and running...!*

By 11:00 a.m., the word's spread around; I'm making a killing on Stellar and brokers drop by my desk to get the lowdown.

"Where's it at now? Still moving higher. Great!"

I dial another client, "Stellar's up 10 points and climbing! I'd be a buyer!"

"Buy me $250,000 at the market!" the client orders.

My eyes blaze with excitement and I get the order in as fast as I can while keeping an eye on my own portfolio.

I went all in as soon as my bank loans rolled over this morning. I'm up $21,455 dollars so far.

And this is the twelfth trade I've placed so far in the name for Monique's clients. I need to increase Monique's commissions as this will ensure a "Stellar" bonus. And I needed to keep this job.

For now, I remind myself.

Robbie cheers me on. "The woman of the hour. Pour some water on her to cool her down. One of these days I want to know how you got your ideas."

"My magic pen, Robbie," I say, holding up my fuzzy pen.

He takes out his Mont Blanc. "I'll trade you."

Another broker passes, "Stellar, way to go, but the company has yet to generate any revenues."

"It's a golden treasure. Buy."

Robbie and I watch STLR flash across the ticker +33...

Paychecks are passed around and one is placed on my desk by a passing clerk. I open the envelope and glance at it: $521.00. I can't help but frown. I pull out my notebook and log the paycheck down on my spreadsheet. *Only $257,988 until I'm out of the hole!*

I turn back to the tape as Stellar crosses +37.13. A flash of arrogance crosses my face and the closing bell sounds. Stellar closes up 35%! "That was good! Dealer wins again!" Robbie and I slap hands.

Phillip, the Managing Director, saunters over. "You the guy holding Stellar?" he asks Robbie.

"No. That's Jolette."

Phillip approaches. "Jolette?"

"Yes, sir."

"Nice play. How many shares of Stellar did you trade today?"

"I'm not sure."

"How many?" he repeats.

"Forty million, twenty five thousand."

"Forty million. Wow. That's a killer day. Killer day." He grins. "What's the best way to go about tradin' in that size?"

"The way you don't lose," I reply.

Phillip grins. "Jolette, why don't you join us tonight after work for drinks?"

"Umm...Thank you, Phillip, but I can't."

"Big date?" he asks, jokingly.

"No, just working late on some paperwork."

He nods, then turns to Monique with a look like, 'hang on to this one.'

The phone rings. I grab the phone, mouthing, "Excuse me." I rise, and look over the trading floor. "Nice call on Stellar, Jolette," Jason Stein bellows through the phone.

"Worked out pretty well," I reply, grinning. "I swear, Jason, someday it's going to be me running my own hedge fund...!"

When Monique takes off, I pull up the "Rothman Securities" website. Finding the number to their San Francisco location, I dial. I need more of this. Much more.

"Rothman Securities."

"Noel Sheffield, please."

"Hold the line."

Is this a mistake, calling him?

No. Not a mistake.

You're chasing him...

Not chasing him. Noel Sheffield has what I want...Plus, I'm supposed to "keep an eye on him."

Waiting, I glance up at the TV. CNBC is running a puff piece about a party at Steve Benson's penthouse. People are in formal clothes, including Benson and his wife, holding drinks and eating canapés on a terrace overlooking Manhattan's Central Park. A TV newscaster says, "This years' party-goers pledged over $30 million to the Museum; lured in part by the chance to see stunning renown hedge fund manager Steve Benson's private island..."

Access to Steve Benson and the secrets of the world are yours. He's the king of leverage. charity overlord...

"Noel Sheffield."

My heart almost stops when I hear his voice. Just the way he says his name... "Nice call on Stellar," I murmur, drumming my fingers on the desk.

He doesn't respond.

I try to keep my voice steady. "I want to hear what else you've got, champ, and don't let me down."

"That may cost you."

I can't tell if he's serious or joking. "Cost me what?" I ask, seductively.

"Meet me downstairs, 2:00. I'll pick you up and tell you."

"Won't get out of here until at least six."

"Okay. Six. I'll pick you up then."

He clicks off, leaving me sitting there, my heart racing.

* * *

At 5:50 p.m. I go into the ladies room to put on some light makeup, and at 5:57 p.m., I'm standing over Kimberly with some files. "Today's my day, Kimberly, I get to leave early."

"What? I don't remember you saying anything," she replies inquisitively.

"Really?" I ask, putting much puzzlement into the question.

"No."

Of course she doesn't remember, because I never told her anything. I hand her the files to further throw her off track. "I took care of the CGC Partnership paperwork and managed to clean the legends off of three more distributions."

She opens the file and is impressed. "Wow, thanks, Jolette, you are fast!"

Kimberly and I haven't become friends, we just work late nights and weekends together grinding out the paperwork.

"Hopefully, I'll get out of today's routine dentist appointment just as fast!" I add for good measure. "See you tomorrow, Kimbo!" I cheer, and even I'm surprised at the excitement in my voice.

* * *

Exiting the building, I see Noel already outside waiting for me. He's wearing a power tailored-made suit and his eyes are hidden behind designer shades. He's leaned up against a Lamborghini with an ego that has more horsepower than the Lambo.

I stroll toward him.

His gaze lingers on me. He smiles.

My face becomes flushed and excitement trickles through me. It was an epic day.

Epic.

And if I play my cards right, there will be more epic days.

I approach Noel and as I get closer, I realize that he's not that much taller than I am. "Let's get out of here," I say, catching a glimpse of his license plate: "TR8DER."

"Is that an order?" he asks.

"Yes."

He opens the car door for me and I slip into the passenger seat. "I'm going to take you for a ride and then for a cocktail," he says firmly, closing the door.

You think I'm going to need a cocktail to get through this? I wonder as I watch him walk around the car.

You're going to need a lot of things, my intuition tells me.

Noel gets in, shifts the car into gear, and we take off.

I'm in a good mood. I always am when I make money. After I blew up in the BBBY trade, I placed a few trades with the little money I had left and I was trading scared. Every trade I placed went down, and I'd panic sell at the low, only to watch it run back up again. Then I'd chase. I was doing this over and over again and losing more money, and I was miserable. I was even a joke in the stock message boards.

But today was incredible.

Noel had what I needed.

Noel is my *ticket to ride.*

And all I have to do is play my cards right with him...

The hum of his Lamborghini relaxes me. Arteries of cars and downtown traffic surround us. I am low in the seat and feel like

I'm wrapped in a warm blanket. I turn to Noel. I wonder what his use of me is. *He dates models... remember what Brittany said?*

And he's "a narcissist, a player..." That's what Monique said.

He looks at me, and now he has his sunglasses off, and I can see his eyes. Blue, turquoise blue melting into mine. For a second he looks vulnerable, caught. "What?" he asks, smiling.

"Nothing."

He has total command of his car and it's a turn on. His elbow brushes against mine and it's like ninety volts of electricity plow through me.

"You should be proud of yourself," he says, "Beating the market is a monumental accomplishment."

I can't tell if there's a hint of sarcasm in his voice.

We hear police sirens, and Noel, distraught, looks into his rearview mirror. We see two cherrytops flashing, and I look over my shoulder, then back at Noel, until the police cars pass.

And then: the memory is before me...

I'm in the back of a car gliding its way up a long, winding driveway in the countryside.

I see a flash cut of my mother's hand, holding a bottle of vodka, deftly steering the car, not paying attention. Sarah and I are in the back seat, I'm six years old. I watch as my mother removes her seat belt. Her eyes are just visible over the top of the dashboard. Soft eyes but fearless, as we hear the sound of a violent collision; brakes locking, metal crunching, gravel spitting.

I cringe, remembering.

Pandemonium and terror, just impressions, I see a tree slamming, my mother leaned up against the steering wheel, bleeding. I scream. SIRENS RISE. My father reaches into the car, takes me into his arms.

Coming back into reality, I turn my mind back onto numbers, levels, charts, stock prices, profits, losses, *anything*, willing for it all to go away.

10

Chapter 10

Noel and I ended up leaving the city. The further away we drove, the further my problems got away. About sixty miles outside of the city, he pulls into a desolate parking lot where there's a run down Target center.

He checks his Rolex, and stares straight ahead. I notice his white crisp Oxford shirt and his initials at the cusp; NMS. And if there's anyone who has more on their mind than I do, it's Noel. He looks so far away and distant.

He cuts the engine, and we wait.

I begin to wonder if this Target is going to magically open and Noel's going to take me inside and buy me unlimited amounts of cotton fruit of the loom underwear.

I suppress a grin and turn to him, my temporary white knight in shining armor, and I wonder what's going to happen next.

When I was younger, I had an almost idyllic view of this man. The prince who was going to come and rescue his queen... But as I've gotten older, I've come to know better. I know now that there's no point in looking for your own strength in another person because at the end of the day, you're only left with the stark realization that it was all just a hope, a dream, a fantasy.

And sometimes I wonder why I dream and dream so much, and it's always because the dream, the fantasy, is so much better than the reality. Reality is tough. It's always changing. Caring is expensive.

Detachment is free. It costs nothing. With caring you can go broke, and it gives whole new meaning to the words, *I lost everything.*

Yet a part of me wishes that Noel and I could just sit in this abandoned parking lot forever. Just he and I, and never go back. Never go back to the real world.

That's crazy, you don't even know him, my brain says.

I know him, my heart argues.

I knew him before I was even born.

A huge tractor trailer with American flags on both sides pulls into the parking lot, beeping its horns. Noel gets out, pulls a briefcase from the back, then comes around to my side, "Let's go."

He helps me onto the massive tractor trailer and hands the briefcase to the driver. The driver is very tall, over six feet, and he wears a Grateful Dead T-shirt.

"This is Larry," Noel says. "He's been driving around the clock. This rig carries 250 gallons of diesel and can cover over 2700 miles before he needs to refuel."

Larry starts doing eighty on the open roads north of San Francisco. He pops his head out. "Actually Noel, it's 300 gallons with reserve and we can hit 3500 with the new gas turbine fuel injectors."

"It's so quiet and smooth, I can hardly tell that we're moving," I admire, exalting in the power of the big rig.

Being fourteen feet up above ground is a heady experience and this is a big rig like no other. Top of the line Viking appliances, brass cabinets, and a twelve foot high ceiling with a marble table and six leather chairs.

"At sixty miles an hour with no stops, Larry can cover the U.S. in several days," Noel adds.

He leads me down a tiny hallway that runs the length of the rig. It looks like mission control at NASA. Each area is filled with monitors, touch screens and consoles, recording devices, and trading systems. Thousands of lights flash, and I feel their heat as we pass.

"These are a part of our trading systems," Noel states. "Every millisecond is money and in our world of high-frequency trading, our orders get sent through these line-of-site microwave repeaters and take a direct route so our orders go off first."

"Nice," I say, though I'm not sure who he's referring to by "Our."

"You can't hit a moving target," he adds, cryptically.

Another door slides open, we exit the control hall, and head towards the rear where on a rack is a Neiman Marcus Limited Edition fighter, a Dodge Tomahawk, and two shiny black Kawasaki Ninja's 650 ABS's.

Noel hands me a helmet and some gloves. "These do well over 200 m.p.h." He gives me a jumpsuit and tells me to put in on.

I'm wearing a skirt and blazer and he's in a suit. I am not sure whether he's joking or not.

The truck has started moving faster, and I'm getting dizzy from the motion.

"We're going to get on these bikes, the back door is going to go down, and I want you to throttle the engine and follow me."

"What?"

"Yes, it's fun."

"No, I'm not interested in doing that."

Noel comes closer to me and whispers in my ear. "You saw what Stellar did today, didn't you? How much money did you make?"

He's breathing on me, and I don't like how turned on I'm getting.

"How much money did you make today?" he repeats. "You do want to know what my next stock pick is, don't you?" he asks, putting his hands on my waist. "Go with Cardano. It's going to take off …faster

....than this skirt," he says, and with both hands, he pulls it down.

I'm standing in front of him in my underwear and *thank goodness it's not fruit of the loom because I own plenty of those.*

But Noel doesn't even look down. His eyes stay on mine. "Now put on this jumpsuit, we're going for a ride."

* * *

Minutes later, we're suited up in leather gear, sitting on the bikes, wearing helmets that are equipped with Bluetooths. Our engines are warmed up and we're staring at the rear wall of the big rig.

"Here's what we're going to do." Noel says, his voice coming through loud and clear inside my helmet. "When this back door opens, a ramp will drop. I go, you follow. Just snap the throttle because we'll be hitting the road at sixty-five miles an hour, so be advancing, got it?"

I watch him and nod. I love speed. If we were racing and it was my body versus his body, he would win. He's stronger. But this is a race of skill and risk. And he won't outdo me.

I'm amped. And Noel is just fuel for the fire. "Remember a good rider has balance, judgment, and good timing."

"So does a good lover," I add, kidding around.

Noel grins, "Ready, set, go!" Noel guns the bike, and takes off down an automatic ramp that comes down.

I pop the clutch and go full throttle... First gear, second gear, third... Going 80 mph....100 mph, 125 mph.... *What a rush...150 mph!*

We own the road; the curves are banked for triple digits. This is pure acceleration, pure speed, pure freedom in every sense of the word. The wind screams in my ears, objects fly by, and the thrill of speed overcomes my fear of death.

"You're doing good," he says as I fly past him, and the feeling is incredible.

"Riding faster than everyone else guarantees one thing."

"What's that?" Noel asks.

"That you'll ride alone!" I laugh and speed off.

Curve after curve, we forget the whole entire world and survive the run of our lives.

Rounding another bend, he catches up to me, "Jolette!" he calls into my earpiece. "We're on arrival. We'll enter the big rig while it's still moving."

"What?"

"Yeah. Just glide up the ramp like you're pulling up to your apartment."

"No way!"

"At 65 m.p.h., I do it all the time."

"Seriously?! We're going to drive back onto the big rig *while it's still moving?"*

"Yes. Watch me."

A ramp rolls down, Noel gets behind it, matches speed, then guns the Ninja, coming to a screeching halt in the back of the big rig.

"That's crazy, Noel, I can't do it!" At this speed, forward inertia will be doubled and can propel me through the other side of the rig.

"Well trained reflexes are quicker than luck. You'll be fine. Come on, it's like your driveway at home, hedge it!"

"I don't have a driveway at home!"

"Just don't over throttle or over brake..."

I take a deep breath. Twisting the gears, I accelerate with velocity, fly up the ramp, pull into the big rig, and stop the bike with ease.

Getting off the motorcycle, Noel takes my helmet off, and my long hair comes tumbling out.

"That was awesome! I want to do it again!"

Noel just shakes his head and laughs.

11

Chapter 11

Bouncers guard the coolest place to see and be seen. Hip and trendy, Paragon is the flavor of the month, here today, gone tomorrow.

Two pony-tailed doormen, survey the crowd, admit a select few, and deny entrance to the rest. Noel leads me right to the front, the velvet ropes are unhooked, and we're let right in.

The place is packed inside. Lights flash. Music pulses. We approach the bar. "Tequila Gold, doubles," Noel orders.

The bartender nods and goes off.

I remove my jacket and Noel notices the gash on my arm. "What happened…? To your arm?" he points.

"Oh, that? I was rushing home on my bike because I was long Bed Bath and Beyond when it tanked and I crashed with it. Lost a ton of money…a ton of my father's money."

The bartender sets down two hefty shots. Noel's eyes sweep back to mine. Looking at me with a lazy curiosity, he asks, "Does it hurt?"

"A little." I lift the glass and bring it to my lips.

"Down the hatch."

We down the shot, and it goes right down into my empty stomach.

"You ever trade that stock?" I ask.

"Not lately," he dismisses. "But I have some ways on how you can get that money back."

"What ideas?" I ask, having a burning desire for his information.

We watch the spectacle on the dance floor and keep a close eye on the TV monitors hanging from the walls. A serious faced anchor is reporting market activity, and unlike the others, we are the only ones paying attention to it.

I notice someone standing in the corner watching Noel. He's gaunt, Northern Chinese, hard, almost 6 feet. He wears red shaded sunglasses and a blue suit.

A manager approaches, "Noel, your table is available now in the VIP room."

Noel nods, motions for me to follow. As we make our way upstairs, I catch eyes with the Chinese man once again.

Noel and I are seated upstairs at a back corner table and a waitress arrives to take our order. When she leaves, Noel's eyes bear into mine. His mouth lifts in a tantalizing smile, bringing dimples to his cheeks and an undisguised challenge in his eyes. "Have you ever heard of a small cap company called Sequenom?"

"I think so. Biotech?"

He nods. "Benson holds it in his portfolio. It's a good time for him to pick up more."

"I told you already, I don't have access to Benson."

Noel only smiles enigmatically. "Jolette, does all this begin to suggest to you some kind of… negotiation? There's something you can give to me, and I want to trade for it."

I shake my head. "A trade is never just a trade."

When the waitress returns with our drinks, Noel orders calamari, oysters, and some sliders and when she leaves, he asks, "Benson will be at the World Hedge Forum next month. You going?"

"Whether I'm going or not, Benson doesn't play high risk/reward scenarios. He's interested in good fundamentals."

"Fundamentals are for buffoons named Warren," Noel says, "Sequenom trades only 300,000 shares a day. If you get Benson on board, there's no telling how high it'll go..."

"Isn't that front running?" I ask, well aware of the unethical practice of trading on advance information. It occurred to me that may have happened with Stellar, but if I didn't dwell on it, I wouldn't have to face that reality.

"Front running?" Noel asks, giving me a piercing look. "According to who? The SEC? What a joke."

He opens a mini-computer and moves closer to me.

"Come here, Jolette, you still need to learn a thing or two about this business. You see this chart here? The stock is going to break out, here."

His proximity is overwhelming, electrifying. He pulls my hair aside to see the screen, and it sends chills down my spine.

I get up, frustrated and frustratingly attracted. "My boss won't let anyone near Benson. If she ever found out, I can get in a lot of trouble. I can lose my job."

"It's a victimless crime..."

"What is?"

Noel peers into his drink and then lifts the glass to his mouth automatically. "Knowledge. Of who's trading what, when. I can give you something better than you've ever had, Jolette. You know what that is? Leverage. Whoever has the leverage has the power. But unless you have some big accounts willing to take down size, then you and I are going to have a hard time relating to one another."

The food arrives and neither one of us touch it.

"You're either in the flow of information or you're out. You decide," he says.

I hesitate.

Noel reads me immediately. "You know what? Forget it. Let's go."

He rises.

"Noel. Wait."

He turns.

"If I bring Benson in…what's in it for me?"

"I'm going to take you someplace that very few people know about. But if you come, you have to promise me you'll bring in Benson."

A feeling of danger makes a tight knot in my stomach. "Where is it?"

12

Chapter 12

Ferrari's clog the streets. Waves of hedge fund managers enter and crowd the hallways. Noel and I approach a large metal door to an unimposing brownstone in Pacific Heights.

Wiseguys stand guard inside. They have piercing, cynical eyes. One of them observes Noel, then looks out. An intricate mirror system lets the guards see through the windows with passers-by unable to see in.

"Hey Dominic."

Dominic nods at Noel and then he looks at me. "Hope you don't mind me checkin' you for weapons." He's tall and muscular with dark hair and skin. Rough-looking.

"It's okay, Jolette,"

I spread my legs, lift my arms. I'd rather not, but there's no choice.

"Nice body," he says, as he pats me down.

"That's enough, Dominic!"

Noel leads me down a long, dark hallway and, out of no-where, Paul Zucker appears. "It's going down tonight."

"Says who?"

"A reliable source," Paul replies, and then disappears in the darkness.

Noel takes me through various doors and hallways and we join other groups of men rushing like rats in a maze, all hurrying in the same direction. I examine beige ornate walls, wall-papered with gold trim. Nothing to get my bearings.

We step into an elevator. The elevator reaches the bottom and we're now down in the basement. We keep moving across another long, dark corridor, gradually losing our sight in the darkness. Seeing nothing, I only hear our breathing, our footsteps.

After a moment of no visibility, we're faintly visible again under fluorescent lighting. Walls that are long and narrow take us around corners and through doorways but there's no indication of where we're going.

A startling clank, like a prison cell unlocking, reveals an unexpectedly vast semi-circular room – and –

Holy. Fucking. Shit. This is a massive underground operation. The billionaire's club. The major engine of the market.

The controlling hub of Wall Street.

Hundreds of hedge fund managers and brokers, early twenties, thirties, shrewd eyes behind glasses, listen to a presentation. It's filled almost entirely with men. The impressive mien of earned authority.

Standing in front of a podium, a well-manicured hand tightly grips a Mont Blanc pen, pointing to assets listed on the board

"That's Rick Tucci," Noel says, quietly.

I nod. He's hard, looks like the smartest guy in the room, compulsively established with haunted eyes. "You want to know the difference between JKR Technology and the Titanic?" Rick asks. "The Titanic had a band."

There's rumbling, murmurs around the packed room. "That's right. Stock's going to hell and we're takin' it there."

Beside him is his analyst, Thomas Wheeler, a young kid with killer confidence, coked out. "We want short sellers only. Name of the game, short and dis-tort. We have Victor at Feldman Brothers and John at

Cadence putting out sell recommendations. Noel will hit the online boards, and I'm releasing a press release with bad news. The data will be run on the dark web in the same marketplaces used for contract killings, sex slaves and child porn."

Noel whispers, "This puts heat on the stock so it moves in our direction."

"Lastly, we're big buyers in two names. You'll be notified tomorrow morning at 4:03 a.m. via text. Use the disposable phones...and remember do not trade these names in your PA."

There are over one hundred suits gathered around tables. Eyes dead as a shark's.

"Lastly, these are the NFT's we're pulling rugs on," Rick says. Some art appears on the screen. He observes everybody in the room and our eyes meet for a fleeting second. I experience a full-body shiver. He has the coldest eyes I've ever seen.

Various computers and control stations are outfitted with super-tech panels to process the avalanche of information.

And as I take all this in, I am absolutely floored.

* * *

"You want something to drink...?" Noel turns to the bartender, "Give me a beer and a soda for her."

We're in a dimly lit private room in another area of this club. "Earnings don't mean anything, revenue doesn't mean anything, cash flow doesn't mean anything. Does it, Noel?"

He knows exactly what I'm talking about.

"The reason why we tell a client to "buy the stock" is not because the valuation long term is sound, but because there's market momentum."

He faces forward, jaw tight, mind working. "We're riding a wave. As long as we get our clients out before the wave crests, we've made them money and have done our job. Capitalism is an astonishingly efficient system."

"And it's the insiders who win."

"Well...you're inside now," he says, low voiced.

"It's not about researching good, honest companies and investing in their future, is it?"

"It never was. It's a zero sum game. One side wins. The other loses."

"But playing games with the market and calling these games investments should not be allowed."

"All aspects of life require a measure of risk and reward. Be informed and make good decisions about your tolerance for risk. If people can't stand the downside, they shouldn't be in the market. Period. The problem is not about the market, it's about understanding yourself."

I shake my head. "The retail guy doesn't stand a chance, Noel. This is Russian Roulette."

"If that's the way you want to look at it, fine, but you can't stop the world because you want to get off. These networks are a part of many industries and they're here to stay. What Wall Street wants, Wall Street gets," he concludes, and he looks around. "Wait here. I'll be right back."

He leaves me sitting at the bar and heads to a back table where Rick sits with Thomas, Dominic, and two other hedge fund managers.

Noel shakes hands with Rick and points to me. He appears taller and darker and more domineering in his masculinity than ever.

Rick looks at me with leering eyes.

I sip my soda and watch the two guys Rick was talking to leave.

Noel returns and says, "Okay. Come on."

I arrive at Rick's table and Noel introduces us. Rick affects an incredibly brotherly tone, smooth but also intimidating. "Sit."

I sit opposite of him. Noel sits beside me.

"So, you're a friend of Noel's?"

"Yes."

"And how do you know each other?"

I look to Noel. He jumps in. "Through Paul."

"Uh huh… And you're looking to trade with us?" Rick asks.

"Yes."

"And where were you working before?"

"I was a day trader."

"What happened?"

"I blew up."

"A maverick then?"

"No."

"You won't have a problem taking our directions, our orders?"

"No."

Rick takes a beat, examining me. I don't flinch.

"She has access to Benson," Noel says, matter-of-factly.

Rick paints a smile over his face. "Okay then…We're going to give you several reports to take down to him in New York. Once you arrive, you will be met by our people there. You'll develop the relationship, deliver the reports, and in five, six days you'll be back here with all your money."

"How much do I get?"

"A hundred thousand for every block of a million shares that Benson takes down."

"And if I get caught?"

"And why would you get caught?" Rick asks, smiling at me caringly."Unless you go to him trembling like a leaf. But no worries, Benson and his team, they don't know a thing."

His eyes narrow. "But once your decision is made, there's no turning back. We know where you work. We know where you live. Understand?"

I stare at him, hesitant.

"If you do anything to screw up our operation, Jolette, you won't wake up in the morning."

He slides a wad of bills across the table. The guard, Dominic, watches, with his arms crossed against his chest. "No strings. Take it…" His stare alters from boyish to demonic.

I stare at the cash on the table.

Money always talks in the most persuasive voice. *Put cold hard cash down on a table and few people can resist picking it up.*

I look at Noel, and then I reach for the cash on the table.

* * *

"I need to get to Izzy's—"

I'm staring at my phone and Noel and I are standing in the middle of the street in Pacific Heights. "I need to get to Izzy's right now!"

"What? Why? Who's Izzy, your boyfriend?"

I pace around, looking for a cab. "I need to get a cab. Where can I get a cab?"

"There are no cabs here." He looks at me lovingly, and pushes the hair away from my forehead. "I'll take you wherever you need to go. Come on. Get in."

We get back in his car. "Please take me to the Marina."

He nods. We drive for a moment in silence. "Why did you take me there?" I ask.

"…You wanted to come."

I stare out the window, and don't say anything.

"Our Triad yields the most powerful men in the world, Jolette. We run everything from Congress, CNN, the global banks, the UN, governments. We fix elections, the World Series, Academy Awards, six Super Bowls… and most importantly… the stock market…"

He puts his hand on my knee. "You're smart. You did the right thing by joining me today."

I push his hand away. "I guess greed always finds a way to get around the law."

"Steve Benson holds the ticket. And you're the one with that access." And then he tries again. The knee thing. With his hand. I push him away, on the verge of hitting him.

"What's wrong?"

I don't answer.

"Do you trust me, Jolette?"

I feel sick.

"Do you?" he repeats, turning to me, "You're in the car with me, so you must trust me. Maybe you even like me? A little bit, huh?"

He turns onto Chestnut Street and I see the bar up ahead. "There it is. Pull over."

"Answer the question."

I turn to him. "I'm with you for one reason, Noel, your stock tips, that's it!" I get out of the car and rush into Izzy's.

Looking around, I head for my brother who's at the end of the bar, drunk. "Yes, I guess he just had a little too much to drink," I say, putting my purse down, smiling uncomfortably. "Thanks for the concern. Sorry again this happened. C'mon Troy." I wrap my arms around him and try and lift him off of the bar stool.

Troy holds on to me, and together we start to walk out.

"Hey, wait a minute!" the bartender calls.

I turn.

"He owes us two hundred and fifty dollars for the drinks!"

I reach into my pocket, hand over Rick's cash, and carry my brother out.

* * *

Outside on the street, Troy can barely stand on his own and his legs are like rubber. I hear the sound of a Lamborghini, and I look up and Noel is coming back down the street.

He observes this pathetic sight and jumps out of the car. "Jolette!"

He runs over to take the other side of Troy. "Bring him to my car!"

"No! He only lives a few blocks away."

"Wait here!" Noel commands. He gets in his car, puts it in reverse, and then drives closer to us.

He gets out and helps me move a limp, wasted Troy into his car.

The next thing I know, I'm wedged in the passenger seat sitting on my brother's lap and Noel is driving again.

"I want to go dancing...Remember the way Mom used to dance? Remember how she loved Barry Manilow... Copa...copa cabannna..."

He pets my hair. "You look just like her, Jo. Jusslikemom... JusslikeHer," he slurs.

I look at Troy and I feel for him. I gently rub my brother's back. "Just hang on, Troy, we're almost home."

I turn to Noel.

He's watching this. There are no words. There is no answer.

And then Troy says, "I think. I think I'mmmm...."

Oh, no.

"I think I'm ... Oh God."

And then, Troy vomits all over Noel's Lamborghini. His mumbles are now incoherent, except for, "Jolette'll clean it up."

Noel looks at me and I'm so embarrassed, my body's subtly shaking from a cry.

* * *

My brother is on all fours, his thin frame is heaving. Bottles are everywhere. I reach for a towel and wipe his mouth in his bathroom.

After a few minutes, I walk out into the living room and Noel is standing by his coffee table. There are framed photos of our family and the twins, and another photo of me and my father, arms around each other, smiling.

Noel has his phone in his hand, and it looks like he's snapping photos.

"What are you doing?"

He spins around, almost caught. "Nothing. Everything okay?"

I'm standing there holding the rag that my brother just threw up in, and I glare at him. I hear my brother calling my name again.

"I'm gonna go," Noel says, "Call me if you need anything."

I rush back into the bathroom to tend to Troy, and barely hear Noel leave.

13

Chapter 13

"GET MOVING! TIME IS MONEY, PEOPLE! LET'S GO!"

The Dow opens 440 points higher and Nasdaq, 380, and the trading floor is complete mayhem. Monique looks around; everyone's hustling, but it's not fast enough.

I hit more numbers on my computer; everything is automated. A hit of the wrong button could be disastrous.

"Come on!" Monique repeats, her face brimmed with panic. "Someone answer line five!"

I grab it. "Trading!"

"Is that you, Jolette?"

"Yes, Brett," I reply, recognizing his voice immediately as I should. Brett is a clerk representing an East Coast Pension Fund, one of Monique's largest accounts. Having no weight of his own to throw around, he takes full advantage of the weight that the account represents. "How can I help you?"

"Are the new accounts opened?"

"Did you overnight the paperwork?"

"Yep."

"Well, we haven't received anything yet," I say honestly.

"Are you *sure?*" he asks with a stifled sigh that only irritates me. "I'll check the files again. Hold the line, please."

I place him on hold and walk over to the filing cabinets. I notice that one of the Benson files is unlocked. So much time has been spent on them because of Monique's pernickety fussing and obsessive nature. I peek in and look at some of the documents marked "CONFIDENTIAL." I also see Benson's cell phone number written at the top of one of the files and I take a mental snapshot of it.

"Jolette, what are you doing?! Nobody is allowed near those Benson files!" Monique splutters. She gets up and slams the cabinet shut, then locks it with a key that hangs on her necklace. "Nobody!"

I flash her a radiant smile. "I know, Monique. I'm just looking for the Toft Pension paperwork. Have you seen it?"

"Ask Kimberly!"

Kimberly is on the phone with another client and I return to the line with Brett. "I can't find it but I'm going to keep looking, Brett. Can I call you back?"

"Fine, Jolette. But we're considering moving our account over to Rothman. It should not take this long for you to get our paperwork together!"

Move the account, Brett. Like I give a shit. You are nothing more to me than a pain in the ass.

Almost psychically, Monique picks up the phone. "Brett, is that you?"

"Yes, thank goodness, *it's you,* Monique. What the hell is going on over there?!"

"What's wrong, Brett?" Monique asks in her most concerned voice, as if she has no idea.

"We're having all these problems! Problems we've never had before! The accounts never took this long to open and we need these trades to settle! My boss is breathing down my neck and he's threatening to move all the business to Rothman Securities!"

Monique points to Kimberly and Robbie, and holds three fingers up which means pick up line three: *now.*

I watch as both of them tap on the line and now all four of us are on the call.

"You know Brett, we lost a great sales assistant due to a death in the family and we've been a little understaffed. You've been so patient, so *wonderful.* Give us until tomorrow, and I promise those accounts will open and the trades will clear. Then we'll wire you the funds promptly."

What is she talking about? We don't even have their paperwork yet! And in a few days we'll see settlement? That's impossible!

Okay, Monique, if you say so, but if you take care of us on the Qualcore IPO, well, that'll really make my boss happy."

"Done, Brett. We'll make sure you see plenty of stock on that deal. I always take care of you...don't I?" Monique murmurs seductively.

"Yeah," he replies, sheepishly.

When Brett seems content, we all hang up the phone. Monique throws off her headset in disgust and rises.

Oh, no. Here it comes. Put your helmet on.

"I want a meeting in the conference room, everyone! Now!"

The three of us get up, file in, and Monique slams the door shut so hard the glass nearly shatters. Everyone on the trading floor watches as another embarrassing scene unfolds.

"What the hell is happening?!" she fumes. "The University is one of our biggest accounts and we're about to lose it to Rothman!"

Don't speak, don't move, don't make a sound. Monique is going to blow.

"How is this happening?!" she gasps. Her face is bright red and her hands are clenched in tight fists.

She fixates her eyes, now narrow slits of fury, on me. "Jolette, who's responsible for this?"

I want to defy her and say, how the hell am I suppose to know? But all I say is, "Monique, I'm not sure. We'll have to go back and check the files.

"You do that, Jolette. Check your fucking files! In the meanwhile, open up a DVP account for the client. Use a fake tax ID number. Clear those trades immediately so we can wire the funds."

Oh, great, more manipulation of account documents. When are we all going to get disbanded from the industry?

After she blows her top and the onlookers on the trading floor have a good laugh at our expense, I exit the conference room with the others.

And then she calls my name, "Jolette?"

I turn.

"You're not going to make it here. And I'd start pulling your weight around here," she threatens. "For every one broker we have working here, there's a hundred who'd kill for your job. And if you can't follow that, follow this," she continues in the same venomous hiss, "Increase your sales quota by the end of the quarter, or else your career here at this firm is history."

I nod, consumed with so much anger and frustration, I want to scream.

* * *

After work, I go over to my brother's so I can check on him. He's on his couch under his blankets, and he looks up at me helplessly. He threw up in his bed sheets last night and slept on his couch.

I do his laundry, put fresh sheets on his bed, and then I wash some of his clothes and underwear.

I wanted to see Brittany; I've barely had time to see her since I started this job, but my hands are full with my brother and I'm too embarrassed to tell her what happened. Plus, she has a crush on him like most of women.

I fold his laundry and think about Monique and what a loose cannon she is. I cannot afford to lose this job. Not until I earn my father's money back. If I just stay the course, everything will work out, I tell myself.

My brother's voice jars me out of my thoughts. "Was that Noel Sheffield over here last night? Or was I dreaming?"

My ears perk up at the sound of Noel's name. Troy remembers.

I nod.

"What are you doing with him?"

"We're working together."

"Working together?! How is that possible? You're a lowly assistant, and he's the master of the market, as they say."

I get up with his clean T shirts and underwear and put them in his bureau. "He has something I want," is all I say.

"What's that?" Troy asks. He sits up, glaring at me. "Answer me, Jolette. Noel Sheffield is not somebody to be trusted."

"Why not?"

"Because he's a user."

I don't say anything.

"It was her birthday, Wednesday," Troy says out of no where. He staggers off the couch and stands in front of me."You remembered, didn't you?"

I want to ignore him, but he keep pushes.

I nod.

"So why didn't you say anything? Why don't we ever talk about it?"

If my brother's trying to get me to leave, then he's succeeded, because I'm out the door.

14

Chapter 14

I spent all day Saturday on my couch watching reality TV, and dined on spaghetti with homemade sauce that I made. The secret ingredient to the best sauce on the planet is Contadina tomato paste with water, cayenne pepper, and sugar. For dessert, I ate Oreo cookies and mint chocolate chip ice cream.

Feeling rested, on Sunday, I rode my bike over the Golden Gate Bridge to see my father.

When I arrive, the door to his houseboat is ajar and I enter… "Dad?" I walk around looking for him. "Dad…it's me."

I keep searching. I can't find him anywhere, and start to get nervous. Walking through his entire boat, I finally see him. He's slumped over his desk that faces a wall, and I hear him weeping.

My heart sinks."Dad?"

I come closer and he's going through a stack of bills.

"Be with you in just a minute, Jolette," he answers, in a strangled voice.

I turn away helplessly, my own grief rising up so rabidly, I find it hard to breathe. I sit down at a table and wait for him.

He finally surfaces from his cave-like office. His face is puffy, his eyes are red.

I stare at him in disbelief. "How are you, Dad?" He sits down across from me. It's as if a part of him died. "Are you okay?" I ask.

"I'm fine."

He looks vacant like his mind is weighed down with grief. Tears began to spill down my cheeks.

I've never recalled a more awkward moment between us.

Sarah and the twins come barreling through the door breaking the leaden silence. "Aunt Jolette's here!"

Sarah's eyes drift to mine and drive through me like daggers. "What is *she* doing here, Dad?"

My father rises. "Sarah ...calm down."

"Calm down, Dad!? How can I calm down?!" Sarah turns to the twins, "Go and wait for Mom outside, please, I need some private time."

Disappointment washes over their faces and they hurry out the door.

"Well, Dad, did you tell her?!" Sarah fumes.

"Not yet."

"So she doesn't know?"

"Know *what,* Dad?" I look at them waiting for an answer, and an aching emptiness engulfs me. "Somebody tell me!"

"I'm here to pick up Dad. He's moving in with us. The boat is malfunctioning; the heater went out and Dad has been freezing at night. I brought him comforters and a heated blanket but nothing works. He doesn't even have water."

"Ohmigod, Dad!" I cry, turning to my father. "What happened to the heater?"

My father shifts nervously, "Well, I was *going* to get it fixed," he says, and his voice trails off.

"Only now he doesn't have the money!"

I reach for his hand and he pulls it away. I whither like grass. Sarah embraces him, and my father practically collapses in her arms.

As Sarah hugs my father, she looks over his shoulder for the twins. "Jolette, go outside and find Devin and Dan while I help Dad with his stuff."

"Did you begin packing yet, Dad?" she asks.

He shakes his head, "No," as if he doesn't even know where to begin.

Stunned, I stagger out the door. Blinded by tears, I wonder if he will ever speak to me again.

I find the twins sitting at the end of the dock. The sun, which has just come out, is now setting, and we observe a Western sky that's turning peach and sapphire.

I sit down between them and strive to control my emotion.

They're chattering away but I don't hear anything.

Devin climbs onto my lap. "What's wrong, Aunt Jolette?" His small skinny arms go around my neck and he nuzzles against me affectionately. "You're still coming to our Career Day, right?"

"Yes, of course I am. November 17th. I wouldn't miss it for the world."

They both hold an expression of trust in their eyes and their smiles are so sweet.

My father and Sarah come outside and stand beside us with two suitcases.

"Let's go boys," Sarah orders.

Devin and Dan get up and go with their mother. "Bye, Aunt Jolette."

Frozen where I sit, I watch them go in the worse sadness of my life.

* * *

I ride my bike as fast as I can, trying to get away from something, anything, maybe especially myself. I head over to another neighborhood, much nicer than my own.

I stare at the starter castle with sweeping views of the Bay. Inside, Noel glides down his staircase wearing a bathrobe and his huge black German Shepherd, "Shep" is beside him.

As I come closer, I can hear him on the phone. "I'm seeing the CEO of Adventure World, he'll be good for another million shares, then I've got Penn Brothers in for fifteen.... Just give me more time! I need another week!" Each pause is more painful. "She'll get to Benson. Once he's on board with Sequenom — we're set!"

I feel like somebody's watching me, and I turn around. No one's there.

I wonder if I should just leave.

Instead, I ring Noel's doorbell.

He passes a towering fish tank, and with two phones in his hands, he moves to the door, and opens it.

"Hi," I say.

15

Chapter 15

Noel's house is spacious though vacant feeling, with massive 30 foot exposed timber beams, multiple skylights, and white washed ceilings. There's panoramic views of the Golden Gate Bridge, and everything is controlled by his smartphone, all the way down to his biofuel fireplace and coffee machine.

"Where have you been?" he asks.

"I had my phone off. What's the big deal?"

He glares at me. "I wanted to see how your brother's doing."

"He's fine. I'm sorry about what happened to … your car."

"Don't worry about it."

"Noel," I begin, "I need to know, what's the trade for tomorrow?"

He turns away. "You're not getting any trade information, Jolette."

"Why not?"

"You know why! The clock's ticking! You need to get to Benson! I took you in! I paid $300,000 for your buy in into the Society."

"What's the trade for tomorrow, Noel?" I repeat, getting impatient.

"There's a process here, Jolette. You need to be bringing something to the table. That thing is Benson. I took a chance on you. And now I'm getting heat. You need to come through for me."

"I'm thinking of going long Tesla tomorrow. I want to buy the options. The chart looks good and you know... Elon..." I start pacing. There's a desperation in my voice and I'm sure he can sense it.

"Tesla? You're going to play the options? Are you crazy?!"

"Why not, Noel?! I like the chart! He's putting people on the moon! The stock is going to catapult!"

Noel shakes his head in disbelief and then walks closer to me like he wants to shake me. "You can't just put your money into something because you like a chart, Jolette! That's not how it works!"

"Oh, no?! Well, it should work like that because it used to!"

"The street is run by machines. You need to get that through your head. The algos control everything. You're on the institutional side of the business so wake up. I need to get dressed now. Decide what you're going to do," he concludes, and walks off.

I've never been to New York and I'm not a fan of big cities. Born and raised in Marin County, I never even left the state. *Why would I? California is beautiful.*

I try to breathe evenly, to have control over one little thing. I see Noel's basketball court outside, and beside the court is a barbeque area with the Bull outdoor gourmet grilling island made with galvanized steel.

There's a stack of ten flat screens on his desk in the center of the room, and I can hear the humming power of his machines. I'm sure Noel trades for his own account, marching from victory to victory with his vast information.

Sitting alone, I wait for him. I fold my hands in my lap and stare straight ahead. I'm afraid. Not so much of Noel. But of myself. There's a sexual tension that's always present whenever we're together. And I won't risk emotional upheaval. Only in trading am I prepared to gamble.

Noel returns from the kitchen wearing a blue Brooks Brothers oxford and khaki's. He has two cocktails in his hands and a file full of research reports under his arm.

He hands me the files and sits down, easing his head back in the soft cushions. Taking in the market news, he mindlessly pets his German Shepherd, who is always beside him.

My eyes fasten on Noel's face.

So many things run through my head. Some people believe that we go through life meeting the same people over and over again. I believe Noel could have once been my husband, my lover, my soulmate...

He moves closer to me. "Here," he ventures gently, "Take a look at these."

I open the file and lift one report to the next, fluttering the pages between my fingers. My deep absorption in the numbers running in punctilious columns is so complete, I'm only dimly aware that Noel's watching me.

My gaze focuses on the reports and my hand falls lightly on his knee. His face gets flush, and he stares at me in fascination. "That's the P & L for Sequenom. The numbers aren't good, but...well..."

I turn another page or two, stiffening. "That's an understatement. So how long have you been in?"

"In what?"

"Rick's society."

"Few years. A partner of mine made a trading error a few years back. One hundred grand. Back then, that was a lot of money. But now," he drinks, "It's a day's pay."

"So they pick a stock and..."

"They pick a stock and everybody gets on the same side of the trade," he says, finishing my sentence. "They work the message boards, the press... We have about forty percent of the big institutions on board with our information, plus Wall Street's top analysts. That's enough to move almost any stock, any crypto, any time."

"And you feel good about this?" I ask, my full attention riveted on him.

"No better than you did manipulating account documents for Monique."

"How did you know about that?"

"I have friends."

Noel rises and marches off to get another cocktail. "This is a rat race, Jolette, and I'm not in it for the long haul. I'm buying a place in Aspen, a place in New York so I won't have to work market hours, a private jet, and a couple more…" his voice fades. "A couple more *of everything*."

He returns with a fresh drink, his composure restored to its usual cool containment.

There's a long silence with me just taking him in. I notice a streak of stubbornness in Noel, an implacable will; a will to succeed, to win, to have more, and to persevere at any cost.

I recognize that same drive in myself. I find him dangerously alluring, and the searing effect he has on me shakes me to my core.

And there's something else. Something inside of me that has been dead for a really long time is coming alive.

"Go to New York," he orders again in a firm, hard voice. "Get Benson to buy Sequenom. That stock will run up and we'll make money for our clients, ourselves; everyone will be happy."

I get up and saunter about the room. I appraise his objects, examining the photos of his father and mother, and his sister in her wedding picture. "My mother always said happiness was an inside job."

Noel stands beside me, and gently touches my face. "Well, what about you? If you could be anything?"

I turn away, nervous, but find myself opening up to him. "Nothing. I'd simply be. I wouldn't be in chase of something — the next stock play, the next account, the next piece of information, the next score. I'd be able to sit still and for once, the voices in my head would stop long enough so I could just breathe."

"Uh huh. And what do they tell you? The voices."

"A lot of things. That I'm not good enough. That someone is going to take something I have away..."

Noel listens with rapt attention. Although he is almost warming to me, he has reached his intimacy limit.

He turns on the TV, grabs his cocktail, and flops down on a separate couch, all in one fluid motion. Then he says exuberantly: "Go to New York. Go to the World Hedge Forum, land Benson."

"And if Monique doesn't get out of our way?"

"Tell her you have some higher ups who'll want to know about her activities."

He reaches for one of twelve portable phones and hands it to me. "Tell her."

"Okay. I'll do it."

"You will?"

"Yes. I'll go. Now what's the next stock pick?" I practically hold my breath as I wait for his information.

"We need to take care of your initiation first."

"My initiation?"

"Yes. In Chinatown. Do you want to go now?"

Before I can answer, Noel says, "Yes, let's go now."

16

Chapter 16

It is beyond the middle of the night, that time when it seems that there are no rules and everything feels unsafe, and Noel leads me through the crowded streets of Chinatown.

The shrill, saw-like sound of the Chinese fiddles and clarinets play amidst the familiar mah-jong parlors that lie beneath the tiny awnings. Under the strings of red paper lanterns and narrow alleyways, lie Chinatown's tight-knit network of shadowy fraternal organizations.

Every pair of eyes seem to follow me. A sultry Asian woman in a black dress smiles at Noel as we pass. We continue down the crowded streets, and stop in front of an innocuous, run-down storefront.

Walking down the stairs, we enter, and hundreds of Chinese men are playing mah-jong. We move through the packed room, and a beautiful, young Chinese woman, wearing a red dress, stands in front of a black door.

When she sees Noel coming towards her, she opens it and we enter a dark, hidden room. There are thousands of candles and the smell of incense is strong.

Ten young gang members are kneeling down at an altar dedicated to "Tee Lu" and a ceremony is taking place. They are reciting a chant with incense burning and an animal sacrifice of a pig.

The smoke hangs like a veil, blurring the few lights there are. Noel turns to me. "Remove all your jewelry."

"Why?"

"Just do it. We're already late." He holds out his handkerchief. "Give it to me."

I take off my diamond earrings, my cross necklace, my bracelet and he takes them. "You're going to become a member of the Triad… Now go and kneel with the others."

Hesitant, I approach the others and kneel down on random pieces of paper that are on the floor. I slowly start reciting the chant which is written on the wall beside Chinese numerology.

"After having entered the Lu gates, I must treat the parents and relatives of my sworn brothers as my own kin. I shall suffer death by eating dead dogs if I do not keep this oath…"

With the others, I raise my three fingers as a binding gesture. "If I am arrested after committing an offense, I must accept my punishment and not try to place blame on my sworn brothers. If I do so, I will be killed by five thunderbolts…"

The scrolls on which the oaths are written are burnt on the altar to confirm each member's obligation to perform his duties to the gods.

"I must never reveal Lu's secrets or signs when speaking to outsiders. If I do so, I will be killed by myriads of swords…"

We pass beneath an arch of swords and continue to recite the Triad's oaths. Triads use numeric codes to distinguish ranks and positions within the gang. It's all inspired by Chinese numerology and I wonder how high up Noel is.

Our fingers are pricked and I see my own blood. A mixture of wine and blood is passed around. I don't want to drink it and look back at Noel.

He nods. He's standing with a group of Chinese men, and when the ceremony ends, I realize he's talking to the same man in the blue suit and red sunglasses that I saw at Paragon. Noel says something in Chinese, and then shakes their hands.

He leads me into another room where Police mull around using services. This room serves as a base for mah-jong, fan-tan, pai gow, and drug dealing. Noel says in my ear, "Black societies have control over the local markets and receive police protection."

A woman approaches us. "Looking for Crab Lady," he tells her.

She leads us to another back forbidden room. It is very smoky, hypnotic almost. A subculture of a subculture of a subculture. There's a dark red curtain. Candles. The men behind the curtain are muttering in Chinese, angry.

We can't see the Warlord but only hear a woman's voice. Noel bows before the altar. "Been holding Sequenom six days now," she says.

"You're up eight percent."

"You promised us thirty."

"I'm handling it. One more month," Noel promises.

"One more month or both your legs will be broken," she says with cold hatred in her voice.

Noel turns to me, fear in his eyes.

"You bring me that stock at ninety. I give you my money. You make me promises. I don't care how you do it. Do it. Stupid man. Did Benson buy in?"

"Not yet," Noel repeats, "One more month please."

"Or else."

Noel nods.

"Did you see Angela yet?"

"No."

"Go now."

Noel rises, and leads me through a series of underground, secret tunnels that run beneath the streets of Chinatown.

These tunnels are ancient and go on forever and everything echoes. At the end of the various tunnels lie darkened caves. He turns into one, backtracks, and says, "No, that's not it." We turn around and I can barely see him and when I think I see a rat, he takes my hand.

Moving through the tunnels that connect into the interspersing streets and stores above, we keep going until we reach a back, dingy room where a secret ritual is happening.

Chinese workers in underwear/lingerie and high heeled boots, play and dance slowly with their received male customers.

It's a brothel.

A sex-filled soiree. It's so dark, I can barely see my way through it. My eyes focus.

Charlatans and superstitious dilettantes wear capes and hum incoherent words in Chinese. They're shaking a clay pot filled with fire and blood. The air is heavy with more incense. Another Chinese woman bangs on drums, a primal rhythm.

"These séances hold secrets transferred through ages unknown and chains of civilizations. They're known to even move certain markets," Noel states.

Sex slaves sit alone on the floor, motionless and drugged up. An older Chinese woman cooks up Fentanyl as another freebases it in the corner. Groans recede in the darkness.

Noel starts speaking Chinese to one of the girls.

I watch as she hangs onto his every word, then nods. She leads us to the corner where there's a tray. On it is a spoon, different powders, an eye dropper.

She takes a square of aluminum foil and brings it to Noel. He lifts the spoon and dumps powder into it. She stirs in some baking soda, drops of water, and then holds a lighter under the spoon. The substance bubbles, crackles.

We sit down on couches and Noel takes the straw and holds it, inhaling the thick smoke.

He exhales, then brings it to my lips. "Do it."

Passing me the straw, he watches me intensely. I inhale the dark smoke. My eyes lose their focus, then droop to half mast. A sexual response. I feel warm and tingly all over. I never felt so good. I slump against Noel on the couch and he looks at me like he has a crush.

The sex slave runs her hands over her breasts and body.

Noel watches. He's turned on. He's very at home here.

Sex slaves are strung out everywhere, on the floor, on the couches and I watch him take another hit. He passes it back to me.

"Where's Angela?"

* * *

I wake up to a sound. Unison and resounding. Growing in volume.

I open my eyes and I'm lying still in a small circle of light, strapped to a table surrounded by hooded figures. They're chanting. Something's burning through me. I open my eyes and see that my body is pierced with hundreds of acupuncture needles and there's a Chinese woman over me doing a séance.

I thrash against the cot, "Stop! Stop!" Sitting up, I rip out the needles out of me. I look around for Noel."Noelllllll!" I stare into darkness hearing low moans as my world spins.

I lift my head and see him across the room. Noel's on a bed with a beautiful, delicate Chinese girl and she's writhing on top of him. She's moaning.

Their moans continue and they get louder. The girl's body arches forward, inch by inch, trembling, her lips distended. She looks about nineteen. The whole room vibrates with their sexual energy.

They're having tantric sex. Going... and going... Everything moves in and out of focus, as sweat pours off of me.

Their breath is in unison. Rising and falling. Deep and slow.

On the other side of the room, I see Paul Zucker. His flesh is getting speared with large needles and he's being tattooed with the gang logo.

The chant rises in intensity.

I close my eyes again and Noel starts to climax. I look up and two Chinese women go to work like a fine-tuned machine; one pulls the Fentanyl over his mouth so he can take another hit...and mid-orgasm, Noel turns to me and his eyes lock with mine as Angela cries out, "Goh-ohhhdd Noel!" Her mouth flies open emitting an unearthly scream that rattles the room, her fingers digging into his flesh and the chant keeps rising, louder...

There are so many beds, couches, and bathtubs filled with people going at it.

I feel more needles getting pierced into my skin and I.... feel something sensational, and then *everything goes black.*

17

Chapter 17

Rushing through the circular doors, moving through the crowded lobby, Robbie passes me, "Jolette, Monique's lookin' for you! She wants to see you in her office, now!"

I acknowledge him with a nod, and jam into the crowded elevator.

Approaching the doorway of Monique's exorbitant office, I lean in, "You wanted to see me, Monique?" Her office is forty-six stories high and so spacious, you can land a 747 in it. The scale and taste of real wealth.

"Yes, come in, Jolette." Sitting at her desk with her back toward the door, she swivels around in her chair. "Take a seat."

I enter and sit in the nearest chair. "Here we go again. Another situation." Gently, she gets up, walks around me, and closes the door."Yesterday, we duped an order for Benson; we placed a trade twice."

"What are you going to do?" I ask, my eyes following her.

Her face looks unnaturally pale and her voice glitters with apprehension. "Technically we have to buy the stock back, eat the loss. But we're gonna take a huge hit. This is a ruthless business, and as women, we need to stick together..."

"I'm here for you, Monique."

"Willing to go to any length?"

"Of course...my background in technical analysis..."

She sticks her hand in the air, stopping me. "That won't get you anywhere up here. Things are probably a lot different around here than what you're used to..." She turns away, then looks thoughtfully out the window.

"This is a massive error. We'll. Need... To hide... No one can know. Benson will keep his mouth shut. So the buck stops... With us. You'll need to create a dummy account, an offshore account, use a fake pin number..."

She hands me a thick folder. Razor eyes and thin lips, she eyes me cavalierly. A sign next to her reads: PIG GETS SLAUGHTERED.

I open the file and glance it over, silently horrified. "Monique, there's no way we can get this past compliance."

"Just do exactly what I tell you!" she orders, her unease escalating. "Take the folder down to compliance. Transfer the fifty million dollar error into the Phi account. File the paperwork in the cabinet under fiscal year 2019..."

"Fifty-million?! Monique, I think we should talk to management."

"Jolette, cut the crap! We don't have time for management. Your options here, they're going to get smaller very quickly."

"What options?! I'm not hearing any options!"

Monique is incredulous. "I've been covering for you with the Lever account!"

"Wha-at?! That was one misspelled word on an account document!"

"It doesn't matter! What if I didn't cover for you, huh? You think you'd still be around?"

There's this dreadful pause. Contempt under siege. The phone rings; it's piercing, abrupt.

"The faster we deal with this, the easier it is to clean up," she insists, ignoring the phone.

I have grown accustomed to Monique's chronic bending of the rules, but I'm appalled at what she's asking me to do now.

The phone still rings and she waves me off: "Go!"

* * *

I head down to the compliance office and hear someone calling my name. "Jolette!"

I turn around and coming down the corridor is Paul Zucker.

Oh, great.

"What are you doing here?" he asks.

"Just... booking some trades."

"Have dinner with me later. We can get that Cakebread wine you love. I want to talk to you about some ...stuff."

"Can't Paul."

"What's the matter? You don't need my money anymore, so you're going to ignore me? Is that how this works?"

He narrows his hostile eyes. "You still have that little trading addiction, Jo? What did you do ...blow up...again?"

I walk away from him.

"You're nothing but a little bitch!" he calls after me. "You use me only when you want somethin'!"

I enter the compliance office, and I am completely unprepared for what I'm about to do.

18

Chapter 18

Noel has picked me up every day after work for the past three weeks. The underground Society has been growing steadily around the world, and hedge funds in Paris, Stockholm, London, Dubai, and Tokyo were all on board with our information.

Privacy and secrecy were of paramount importance to Rick and we were cornering the global markets. The locations of the meetings were changing on a regular basis, and Noel and I were traveling all over the city.

Upon arrival, we're patted down for weapons. The buzz of what's next and the political wrangling inside the organization vibrates the air like discordant machinery.

Every morning Rick has surveillance experts sweep the area for bugging devices and warns everyone that it's imperative to be on alert. One mistake can blow the whole operation sky high.

This isn't ordinary power.

This is immense power.

The Society has just gone long a company called Finray; we were big buyers. It's a play off of the government legalization of marijuana.

The stock had been hammered in the past, trading as low as 10, and I remembering watching it when it hit an all-time high of 80 in aftermarket trading when they pumped it on CNBC. After that, the whole sector took a dive, and bagholders were plenty.

I was trading Sundial at the time. I rode it from .72 cents to 3.46 and made over $106,000 in that trade. It was incredible. I ended up losing the money just as fast, but that's another story.

Besides, those days are over. I'm trading with Noel and the Society now and it's a whole different game. Things are improving. Finray is set to take off tomorrow and it's the same process – somebody would hit the press and stock message boards with positive news, everybody would put their clients in it, and the machines and algorithms would do their work, and Finray would skyrocket.

Ten hedge fund managers and analysts, sleeves furled up, ties crooked, stand at the blackboard with Finray's assets diagrammed on the board.

Up at the board is Rick, who appears more high-strung than usual. "Finray's Canadian operations filed for bankruptcy today, and similar stocks on the Canadian exchange collapsed. Law enforcement is looking into some of the bigger hedge funds who unloaded 800,000 shares thirty minutes before the information went public. Felony charges carry a maximum penalty of twenty years in prison and a forty-million dollar fine. So watch your step..."

I turn to Noel and his hands move from his chin to brushing against his nose, giving the impression of weariness girded by a deeply rooted apprehension.

I hold over 10,000 shares of this in my account. The Society rules were that we weren't allowed to trade these names in our "PA;" our "personal account," *but what did I care?*

There was no greater high than watching my portfolio tick up at work while I was getting beat up by Monique and the clients all day long. Plus, I had my father to pay back.

It had been a good run so far.

I was making bank.

It could only get better.

I felt lighter. Like the monkey was off my back.

For now.

Last week, I wired my father $16,000. It wasn't much, but it was a start. I was holding most of the money so I could keep trading with it. "Doing real well, now, Dad," I told him. "Didn't I tell you I'd be able to make the money back?"

Rick continues, "Word is on the street is that the company's created a web of relationships and has engaged in massive abuse. But the stock is going to run tomorrow. If you're a short seller and alarmed by threats, carry a gun. For the most part, we've covered our tracks. Use the code names and the disposable phones, because this thing is going to rise to 85 by next week. And then we're going to knock it back down..."

His assistant, Thomas, anxious and fidgety, pipes in. "Massacre one stock and you're a slayer. Massacre hundreds and you're a conqueror. Massacre all of them, and you're God."

He grins, maniacal.

I raise my water bottle with the others, and laugh, "To the chosen ones!"

* * *

The next morning, Finray opened at $10.01 and it broke out at 9 a.m. and just kept running. It closed up 36% on the day, and it even traded higher in aftermarket hours.

I made another hundred and fifty grand.

I put Monique's clients in it too... because *why not?* The more investors, the merrier, and Monique loved the extra commissions I was bringing in. She didn't question me anymore.

No, her attitude has definitely taken a turn.

I'm on the inside now.

People are starting to appreciate me.

And things are about to get massively better.

* * *

Friday night, Noel and I went to dinner. We were sitting outside at McCormick & Kuleto's in Fisherman's Wharf, and the sun was just setting. It was the middle of October and the weather was cool, and so was Noel's attitude toward me.

He never made any kind of a move on me and I felt more like his sister than anything.

But I was fine with that. I enjoyed hanging out with him but more than that, I loved what he brought to my life.

I have been doing a lot of thinking, and have been giving my trading habits a lot of thought. I decided that once I made my money and paid my father back, I wanted to get more conservative, even ease up on some of my trading activities.

"I …"

Noel looks up from his crab cakes, "You what?"

"I asked my father today for his broker's name… and … well, once I pay him back, I want to put my money over there. You know, stop trading for a while."

He nods. He doesn't really want to hear it.

"But my father won't give me the broker's name."

"So you can use anybody," Noel says.

"Not anybody I can trust. My father has always been very conservative with his money. And in this current market environment, I don't think that's a bad thing. But I think it's a hold he keeps over me. You know? Never wanting me to be financially independent, so I'm always dependent on him."

"Your father gives you money?"

"Well, sometimes, when I need it."

"Jolette, you need to get to Benson. Then you won't need it."

There he goes with Benson again.

"Did you ever wonder why you have such a reckless relationship with money?" I ask.

He looks at me like I have a thousand heads. "I don't have a reckless relationship with money."

"You take risks."

"My risks are calculated."

He sits across the table from me and appears like the largest piece of stainless steel that cannot be twisted or broken. "What's your father like?"

He keeps eating, doesn't respond.

"I asked you a question."

He looks back at me. "Reactive."

"Reactive?"

He nods but doesn't elaborate.

It's one word but it says so much. "Where did you grow up?"

"New Jersey."

He keeps eating, eyeing me. "How about your Mom?" I ask.

"She's in Florida."

"They're divorced?"

He nods. He doesn't want to talk about anything. "I'm sorry," is all I say.

"It's for the better," he adds. "My father runs. He's a runner. And that's never the answer to anything. It taught me a lot. Where did you grow up?"

I point across the water. "Right over there, Marin county." And then I ask him. It's been on my mind and I couldn't stand it anymore. "Why did you sleep with her?"

"Who?"

"Angela, in front of me?"

I have swept that whole Chinatown experience under the carpet and we never talked about it. I just saw it as something that got out of hand and it would never happen again.

And it hasn't.

And it won't.

"Angela?"

I nod. "In Chinatown."

"I never slept with her."

"But I saw it."

"She wasn't even there."

I think about this. *Is he lying?*

"Your mind is playing tricks on you," he says, "Drop it."

I let his words sink in. I'm not sure whether to believe him or not. "And no matter what happens," I tell him, "I am not getting the gang tattoo."

"Tattoo? What tattoo?"

"The gang tattoo. I saw Paul Zucker getting it. I won't get one."

"You won't have to. And Paul wasn't even there that night either."

I stare at him in stunned disbelief. *Was I hallucinating all that?*

"Your mind is playing tricks on you," he repeats. "Drop it."

He finishes his lobster roll and leans back in his chair. "You dated him, didn't you?"

"Who?"

"Paul Zucker."

I tread carefully. "We dated, briefly… It meant nothing."

"That's not his side of it. What really happened between the two of you?" he asks, sitting up in his chair. He seems eager for an answer.

I take a sip of water. "He started with the W's."

"The W's?"

I nod.

"What's that?"

"You know, the W's. Where are you? Who are you with? When are you coming home? What are you doing? ... the W's."

He grins. "Oh. I see."

"Unacceptable."

He nods. And then he laughs. "The W's..."

Signaling for the waitress, he shakes his head, "You really are something else, you know that?"

I watch him and wait for his next words. I realize I'm going to be waiting for a long time because he doesn't say anything. I don't want to tell him what I thought the real truth was and that was this: Men need women. Women need money.

He drops me off at home fifteen minutes later, and yet all I can think of is Noel, Noel, Noel.

When. When. When.

* * *

The next day, I get a text from him, "Had a good time last night."

It was a crazy day on the trading floor, and I didn't get time to respond.

Two hours later, I get another text. "You're on the red eye flight tonight to New York. Pack your bags. I'll take you to the airport."

19

Chapter 19

"I don't understand. You're going to New York. To see clients?"

I stand in my brother's doorway with my cat in my arms. "I told you already."

"Well tell me again."

"I need you to watch Sammy."

"Oh God, you know I don't like cats! What do you know about that, Jolette? The financial world on the East coast —"

"What? You don't think I can handle it?"

"That's right, I don't think you can handle it! Are you and Noel Sheffield involved?"

"No. We're not involved." I walk in and start to set up my cat's litterbox in my brother's bathroom.

"Did you know last year Sheffield came to me and pitched Transun Airways? You remember that company, that defunct airline? I looked into it —they never owned or operated a plane. Never conducted any airline business at all! No revenues – nothing! It was a pump and dump!"

"Troy… stop."

"He has a terrible reputation, Jolette! Need I remind you that mob involvement on Wall Street is not new."

"Mob involvement? Okay, Troy, I work on Mob Street now. Take the needle out of your arm."

"The crime families are switching over! It's all about white collar crime now. Remember, I knew those guys over at Hanover Sterling — the ones who offered that undercover agent posing as a money manager a 25% kickback to take down 2.5 million dollars of that bank stock!"

"Hanover Sterling is yesterday's news. Those are the guys that were so stupid they had to pay imposters just to pass their Series 7 exams. Those were the type of people that you were involved with. So don't talk to me about Noel Sheffield."

"No riff raff at Uncle Troy's!" Sarah says, as she and the twins come marching through the door.

Troy and I look up.

The twins run towards me, they're faces wreathed in smiles. "Hi Aunt Jolette! Look, we have new cards! More tricks!"

I bend down and hug them, and then I rise and go into my purse to remove some coupons to AdventureWorld. "I've been saving these for you, Sarah. More coupons to the park, 20% off."

"The ones you gave me last time expired, Jolette," she states, and hands the coupons back to me.

"What do you mean, expired?"

"We went all the way up there and they didn't even take them. You know we can't afford paying full price at AdventureWorld."

I stand there looking for an expiration date, but I don't see one. "That's weird…"

"Boys, can you wait out in the hall? I need some private time."

When the twins are out of sight, Sarah asks, "What's she doing here, Troy?"

"She's going to New York with Noel Sheffield."

"Noel Sheffield?! Isn't that the guy who blew up Troy in that IPO?"

"He's in the Triad and if Jolette's involved with him, she's in a gang."

"I'm not going with him, and a gang, Troy?! Come on!"

Sarah glares at me.

"The only gang I've ever been involved with is the Girl Scouts!"

"Jolette, what did you do to Dad's money?!"

"I have everything under control, Sarah."

"How?! Dad said you got a margin call! How much money did you lose this time?"

"Sarah, you have it all wrong. Dad and I invested in Bed, Bath and Beyond and it's a solid company. The trade went awry…it wasn't my fault…and…"

"It's never your fault! You're always taking chances!"

"And you've made me pay for every one of them." I walk away from them. I can't take it anymore.

"So now what, Jolette? Has Paul Zucker given you another loan? Is he still enabling your gambling addiction?!" Sarah fumes.

"No, Sarah! I paid Paul back! Everything is different this time!"

"Different… huh? The four most dangerous words in investing and in life are: "This time it's different."

She turns and goes out into the hallway while Troy has that look on his face like: See?

"Boys!?" Sarah calls. "What are you doing? Come back in here!"

They scurry inside and she shuts the door behind them. "Who was that man? Didn't Mom tell you to never talk to strangers?! Who was that man you were talking to?!"

Alarm bells go off. I go out into the hallway to check to see who's there, but whoever it was, they're gone.

I come back inside and the twins look afraid. My cell phone starts ringing, and I have a flight to catch. "Troy, feed him twice a day and make sure he has clean water. I have to go."

"Jolette, when are you going to learn that big money runs the street?!"

"I am big money now!"

Troy follows me downstairs and out onto the street. "Jolette, wait!"

Noel is parked outside in a new Mercedes McLaren. He's on the phone, and I can hear the end of his conversation.

"Why didya have to let Jolette Marco in?! She's green! A noob!" Paul asks over speakerphone. "The clock's ticking, Noel! Rick does not feel comfortable letting someone in that he does not know personally!"

"I have her handled! You worry about Rick and I'll handle Jolette!"

I approach the car with my suitcase and Noel finally sees me. "Rick and I have worked together for five years," he concludes, not realizing that I can hear him. "He wants me, he's got to take her in. I gotta hop."

He clicks off, then gets out of the car. His eyes are concealed behind aviator Ray Bans.

Troy stands there. He and Noel stare at each other. Noel puts my bag in the car, and uncomfortable, I get in.

Noel gets behind the wheel, and rolls up the window to seal me off.

We drive away, and Troy stands there on the street, watching us go. Noel reads my nervousness as he weaves in and out of traffic. "Don't worry."

I turn to him, my eyes serious, as they search his face, now so very important to me, and rarely out of my mind.

"Everything's going to be fine," he adds.

"You know why I like trading, Noel?"

He turns to me. "Why?"

"Because there's no time to stop and think about anything. You're completely immersed in it, almost as if you disappear… "

I loved trading with such an eminent simplicity and I couldn't even imagine a life without it.

He nods. "You know why I like it?"

"Why?"

"Because I never realized that it was possible to feel like both God and the Devil at the same time."

My breath catches in my throat.

He hands me a phone. "Any e-mails, texts, calls to me, use this going forward."

"...What is this — a disposable?"

"Yes. Compliance has been buckling down. They read everything coming in and out to the firm."

"So?"

"So all the phone lines on the floor are tapped. It's safer, saves us any headaches later on. Everyone has one."

I don't argue or question Noel now, I'm merely just a creature at his mercy.

Noel reads a text, then makes a U turn in the middle of a four lane street. Moments later, he pulls into an abandoned parking lot not far from the airport.

"What are we —"

He stops me from talking by putting his fingers to his lips. He's listening for something. I turn to him and his face is covered with a thin film of sweat. He looks unwell and disoriented. "Have you told anyone that I'm here?"

"No."

"Okay. Let's go."

"Noel... are you..."

"Jolette..." he cuts me off. "This is very important. And you must listen. You have to get to Benson. Now go."

We face each other for a moment.

"I will, Noel, don't worry."

We exit the car.

Ahead of us, six men walk towards us in business suits as Rick, Paul and a few other Russians wait in a Cadillac SUV.

Rick gets out, carrying a briefcase.

They approach us and Rick removes a wad of money from his wallet – hundreds.

"The rest will be wired into your account. We set one up for you offshore."

I nod.

"When Benson asks why you've come, tell him you know he's a player in the biotech space."

He hands me some more files. "These are the reports, credit card, your airline ticket. Here's an emergency number."

He writes something on a piece of paper and hands it to me. "And suite nine ten at the Four Seasons. When you arrive in New York, there'll be someone there to meet you."

"How will I know who it is?"

"They'll know you. The key is to stay calm and to play it cool." He leans in, "And if you give them any information about us, we'll deny everything. We know where you live, we know where your family lives. Am I clear?"

He glares at me. His look is chilling.

I walk back to the car with Noel, and everyone drives away…

And …then…

NOEL'S MCLAREN BLOWS UP!

Pieces of his car explode sky high before either one of us know what is happening. I look up at Noel, shocked.

He stands there frozen.

We should be dead.

We're not.

His cell phone rings, he answers: "This is a warning, Sheffield. Sequenom better get to 99 or next time you'll be in that car —"

Noel takes my hand and starts running …I trip and Noel lifts me up into his arms and carries me as the GAS TANK EXPLODES!

He keeps running to the far side of the parking lot and puts me down on a ledge. I'm bloody and shaken and a wave of nausea washes over me.

I slowly open my eyes and I see his face.

Everything's goes blurry, and I close my eyes again and then open them. Things get clear again, and Noel envelops me in his arms. "It's okay now. It's over."

With a sudden tenderness that surprises me, he gently wipes my tears away. "Don't cry… don't."

I gather myself and look at him… trusting him.

We pull apart and stare at each other, unsure what to do about this growing electricity between us.

20

Chapter 20

Noel and I move through the crowded airport that's filled with energy and people, and he stops walking. He leans me against a wall. "You don't have to do this," he says, knocking over my suitcase. Pulling me closer, he whispers in my ear, "Don't go."

I look into his eyes. "I have to now, Noel."

He nods.

We start moving again. When it's time for us to separate, I hear him say, "Be careful," but I don't turn to look at him, I just keep on going.

* * *

A deafening roar as the airplane, a 747, ascends into the night sky...

I lean my head back in the business class seat and all I see over and over again is that explosion.

My ears are ringing, my lip and forehead is caked with dry blood, and a stewardess approaches and hands me a warm cloth.

I thank her and when I bring it to my face, it stings. She asks if I'd like a drink and I order orange juice. I have to hit the ground running when this bird lands at 6:00 a.m.

I told Monique that I would attend our firm's annual medical conference in New York to get her off my back. But I had no plans on attending.

What I do plan on, is selling her clients on Sequenom. The more investors I plow into this, the more it should run up. I'm holding 5000 shares in my personal account.

And I need a score.

The stewardess puts a piping hot meal in front of me an hour into the flight, and I enjoy barbecued chicken, mashed potatoes and spinach. I'm so happy not be rushed or surrounded by people where I have to make innocuous conversation. I don't even have to move for the next six hours, and I take great solace in this fact.

Once I'm in New York, it'll be a different story.

I need to get to Steven Benson, the world's most powerful financial titan running the largest hedge fund known to man, and *sell him.*

When I finish eating, I lean back, close my eyes, and all I see is Noel.

Manly, stoic, Noel.

He rides the gravy train well…

And everybody wants to come along for the ride.

21

Chapter 21

I move briskly through LaGuardia Airport terminal carrying my briefcase, and I scan the crowd for my contact. My arm is grabbed by a wide-bodied, narrow-eyed man in his late sixties wearing a dark suit.

"Follow me," he says, low-voiced, his eyes darting this way and that. He takes my brown leather tote bag and leads me outside to a parked Maybach.

Opening the car door, I step inside, and the man disappears.

The Maybach races over the Whitestone Bridge, as the sun rises. The car has a voice-activated power panoramic sunroof, and the glass windows are heated.

The driver looks leery and keeps staring at me, and I realize he can drive me anywhere, have his way with me, leave me for dead, and nobody would notice. *Would anybody care?*

I try not to think about it.

The driver speeds through the highways with professional care, and I focus on my surroundings. I observe the epic span of the Triborough Bridge and the East River. The clear turquoise sky is the perfect backdrop for a day in New York City. The huge skyscrapers appear to sparkle. This city holds all the promise and mystery in the world, and it's known to have *everything.*

We enter Manhattan, and traffic barely moves, a bicycle messenger flies past, a cop disappears into an underground parking structure. People hurry down the streets amidst the high-rise buildings, buses stop, horns beep, and there's the human gridlock of Fifth Avenue. I take it all in, mesmerized.

The Chrysler Building shines and colorful graffiti over buildings read: "Smoke Crack, Worship Satan." It's sensory overload, addictive, hypnotic. A bum holds a sign: THE END IS NEAR.

The Maybach pulls up to the Four Seasons, and when I walk inside, I marvel at the marble floors, high ceilings, and service that's impeccable.

I'm escorted to my room, tip the bellman generously with Rick's cash, and when he leaves, I walk over to the windows. There's a beautiful view of Central Park and the leaves on the trees are just turning beautiful shades of purples and reds. Reaching for my phone, I snap some photos and send them to Sarah. "Show these to Devin and Dan. This is Central Park!"

I put my phone down and need to get moving. I take a shower, put on a suit, and I'm downtown by 7:45 a.m.

I step out of the SUV that the Four Seasons provided, and Wall Street roars to life.

Hundreds of businessmen and women rush through the surrounding maze of streets all in pursuit of one thing: money.

My first meeting is with Ojai Advisors, a 600 million dollar hedge fund, small by Society's standards, but Jason Stein worked there and he'd be an easy kill.

He made bank on Stellar Blockchain and he'll take down an even larger block of Sequenom. He's also active in some altcoins and NFT's and I'll give him a taste of those Society names as well.

I enter 23 Wall Street and announce myself to Security. They need to take my photo and I step in front of a camera and smile.

They hand me a badge, escort me into the elevator, and hit the button for the 18th floor. I notice the other people in the elevator and they appear more serious than California. They're more stern, more hurried. Nobody is tan or smiling, and everybody's wearing dark clothes. Dark coats, dark suits. Dark. *It's all dark.*

When the elevator opens, I whisper, "Showtime," and step off.

Announcing myself to the receptionist, she escorts me into a large conference room. "Jason and his team will be with you in a minute. Would you like coffee or water?"

"Coffee would be lovely, thank you."

Checking my phone, the market still hasn't opened yet, but Sequenom is trading 2% higher in pre-market trading. I keep watching it. Every tick that it moves up gives me a little jolt. I wish I could watch it all day, but I have sales presentations to nail.

I take out my laptop and plug it into their video conference machine so the clients can see my charts and graphs on the big screen. I place printed presentations at every empty chair, and I start to play some music from my laptop because I like to create *a vibe.* I take a moment to center myself, and when they walk in, I'm on fire.

Introductions are made, everyone is seated, and I begin my presentation strong.

My tight little body is a crème Calvin Klein suit and a white silk blouse that has a bow on it that I bought online from a store in London. It's beautiful. My heels are high, but not too high, and I always wear pearls. I look professional and classy.

A turned on man can quickly become a frustrated man and I didn't want that. These are America's premiere alpha males, the world's exclusive power players, and there's a time for seduction, but this is not it. As a woman, I understand the power that I have over men but I strive to exude an energy whereby I'm just seen as the female version of one of them, and therefore they're engaged in what saying and more importantly, *what I'm selling.*

I am on point and in control with high energy and I don't stop until I jam whatever stock it is that I am pitching down their fucking throats. *Any questions?*

No, I don't think so because I covered every base.

I wrap it up quickly because everybody wants out. Get in and get out; just be quick, move it along and get to the fun stuff, whether it's the breakfast or lunch that I've ordered in, the reservations I made at a restaurant, or tickets to a sporting event, concert... whatever it is – just keep it moving.

Because remember, *you can't hit a moving target.*

At 8:45 a.m., breakfast arrives and everyone gathers around the food to eat.

Jason Stein approaches and shakes my hand again, smiling, "Thank you, Jolette. That was great."

I nod, pack up my things, and do it again.

* * *

And again.

And again.

* * *

By 7:00 p.m., I finish my final presentation.

That evening, a limousine races along the West Side Highway, dwarfed by the city's spectacular skyline. I sit with eleven alpha males, mid-twenties, fashion slaves, holding cocktails. One client lights up a cigar. Another does coke on a mirror.

CHAPTER 21

I hold a glass of Chivas and as the alcohol trickles through me, my anxiety slowly subsides.

The clients appear less hostile, less intimidating, and my smile is superior. I know that taking these various clients out to dinner and wherever else the night may take us will pay enormous dividends.

I've decided to establish attitude and position from moment one so I sit back quietly, watching, feeling like a reluctant, but accurate observer of life's great charade.

The car weaves in and out of traffic and the concrete jungle comes alive. Thousands of tiny New York City windows are lit up and look like a million sparking diamonds.

The neon signs and giant billboards illuminate Times Square, and the bars and clubs are packed with people.

Downtown, an endless stream of taxis and limousines pour into the narrow streets of the East Village. We enter a trendy restaurant, and the decor is a mixture of chi-chi and nouveau riche. White silk curtains, handwritten menus and lavender tablecloths are decorated with arrangements of exotic flowers.

Huge white porcelain plates displaying tiny, elaborately decorated appetizers are placed down on our table. The clientele is young, wealthy, confident, dressed in slinky Prada and classic Armani. There's cryptocurrency traders. Money managers. Influencers.

Laughter grows as the night carries on. More bottles of blue-chip burgundies are set on the table.

Dessert arrives and it's a massive piece of New York strawberry cheesecake. I pick up my fork and dig in, enjoying every bite, and a small smile nestles on the corners of my mouth. *Because if you can't beat them, join them.*

By midnight, we're at an exclusive nightclub and fifteen tequila shots are lined up on the bar."To Sequenom!!"

It's all too much. *Way too much.*

The music blares and half naked women dance in large cages. The bill arrives, and my eyes glaze over as I focus on the tab.

I've had so much to drink, I could blind a small animal. The tab reads: $38,677.98. I reach for the pen, hand over Rick's credit card, and sign off.

Amex Black is beautiful.

I don't return to the hotel until five in the morning and couldn't believe that this New York City lifestyle.

I had a ball, but couldn't imagine living like this every day.

Or could I?

22

Chapter 22

My head pounds the next morning and I reach for my phone in the silence of the Four Seasons hotel. I check Sequenom and the stock is up 6%. *Nice.*

This is going to be a home run, I think.

A home run.

I need some water but first I check my missed calls. Monique has called twice, and Paul Zucker has called three times. Listening to voicemail, Paul says, "Jolette, you're pushing me around like I'm a vacuum cleaner."

I hit delete thinking, *he wishes.*

His next message: "Jolette, you use sex as a tool, and you're a sex maniac." I hit delete again.

Relief comes when I hear the final message: "Aunt Jolette, it's Dan. We miss you. Bye."

I call him back immediately and he picks up my sister's cell. "Hi Dan! How's my sweet prince?!"

"Hi Aunt Jolette, we miss you."

"I miss you, too, sweetie. What's going on?"

"My friend's Dad was going to come for Career Day to talk to us about the stock market but he can't come and I told everybody that you are coming!"

"That's great, Dan! Just great!"

"I know, Aunt Jolette. They said he lost a lot of his money in stocks and coins. You're the stock market queen!"

"Thank you, Dan," I say, feeling sorry for the poor guy who lost his money. *I know that feeling.* "How's mom?"

"Good."

"Can I speak to her?"

"She's in the bathroom doing dumps. Have to go now Aunt Jolette, bye."

He ends the call.

I get out of bed and stare at my reflection in the mirror, repeating Dan's words, "I'm the stock market queen!"

With newfound energy, I run my fingers over the cut that's starting to fade from my face, and I hope that this nightmare just fades along with it.

Today's the day.

Benson.

* * *

I wanted to stop off at St. Patrick's Cathedral on my way to the Hedge Fund Forum so I leave the hotel early. Walking down the crowded streets, I cross over to Fifth Avenue and I find the beautiful, majestic cathedral that sits in the center of midtown Manhattan. It's located right across from the esteemed Rockefeller Center, and I walk inside.

It's so quiet and peaceful, it's like going into another world. I walk through the church in awe, taking in the thousands of candles and the massive altar. I feel so at ease here.

I go into a pew far away from everybody and get on my knees. My prayers always start out for my brother, and then I move on to my dad, and the rest of my family, and when I'm done praying, I sit up and listen to the silence.

The silence reminds me of all the money I lost trading, and I think of how many times I was told a company was solid, or had a stellar future, only to watch its stock crater and be left holding the bag. It was too many times to count. Yet as I sit here in this church, not staring at my phone or computer screen and far away from it all, I finally feel some semblance of peace.

But I know that once I exit these church doors, I'll be back in chaos once again.

And when the music stops, *nobody knows.*

* * *

Fifty-Fourth Street is rigged with black SUV's.

Dudes wearing black shades and black clothes sit behind windows tinted black. Menacing guys, strategically placed with earpieces, all whisper into shirt cuffs.

The Waldorf hotel is overfilled with Wall Street's financial elite. I enter the lobby and it swims in crystal chandeliers and timeless opulence, and I take in the glittering scene at a glance.

People are staring at me and I feel like I'm being followed. I start to wonder if I can even pull this off.

And what if can't?

What will Rick do?

Getting nervous, I turn and go outside for some air. Opening my briefcase, I find my bottle of water and take a few sips. I wish Noel was here with me.

As I stand on the sidewalk, a black limousine pulls up. I watch a man step out, and there's a donut of men surrounding him, protecting him, placating him.

They move quickly towards the entrance, and I see glimpses of a white Hermes scarf... $15,000 crocodile loafers, tailor made Pucci suit, meticulous hair...diamond cuff links...

I see only a partial view of the man as he enters the hotel, and decide to follow.

Waiters and employees are all in a high state of alert. Guards and distinguished executives bow their heads in respective greeting. The man maintains a high rate of speed toward the private staircase.

A security guard exits the stairwell, and immediately afterwards, the man turns.

Now I see him head on.

It's Steven Benson.

He's simply majestic. A Wall Street legend. The whale of all whales. So distinctive and alluring you can spot him a mile away. Unlike any other man in the universe – *unequivocally Benson.*

He steps into a staircase, a Security guard steps out and closes the door behind him.

I realize I can't follow any further, so I turn with all the other suits and make my way upstairs to the main ballroom.

23

Chapter 23

Steve Benson's voice resonates through the hotel corridors. "We're in a Golden Age for Alternative Investments. Capital markets are the lifeblood of the world economy. They're an integral part of our ability to compete globally and we must continue to adhere to an ongoing commitment to our vested shareholders..."

I see an open side door, and stand there and listen. "Defined philosophies and well executed trading processes ensure the integrity of our capital markets."

I watch Steve Benson at the podium and he has full command of the room. "This deserves the utmost protection from fraud and stock manipulation, as well as any other potential systemic risks which must be continuously identified and mitigated."

A woman approaches me with a clipboard, diverting my attention. "Your name, please?"

As I admire Benson's morality towards the industry, I turn to the woman and our eyes meet. "Jolette Marco."

"I don't see your name on my list," she miffs.

"We're going to reform how Wall Street does business and put an end to the greed that has driven our markets into chaos. We'll put an end to multimillion-dollar payouts to CEOs who have broken public trust..."

"What firm are you with?" the woman with an overabundance of hair on her upper lip, nags.

She's a pest. "ABLX Securities."

I hand her my business card, and turn back to Benson.

"We'll put an end to running Wall Street like a casino. We'll make sure your savings — IRA, 401(k) and pension accounts, and crypto wallets are well protected. We will protect all cryptocurrency and altcoin holders and the NFT community..."

Hundreds of heads nod in agreement with Benson.

"Firm *name,* Ma'am?" the woman repeats, this time very loudly.

"ABLX Securities." *It's written on my business card. Are you blind?*

"I don't see your name here...No, your name is not on this list! This is a $45,000 a head luncheon and we cannot let you in!"

Hotel security surrounds me before I can even grasp what's happening. "Come with us," they say, and my thin arms are grabbed and I'm escorted out of the Waldorf Hotel through a back door by Security.

Damnit!

Humiliated, I pace around, trying to figure out what to do next. A moment later, a tuxedoed waiter exits through the same back door.

I reach for the hundreds that Rick gave me. "Hi. I'll give five hundred for that vest."

"Sure!" the waiter replies, and takes it off. "I don't even make that in a week."

I take off my coat, put his vest on over my white blouse, and clip my hair up in a neat chignon. I grab the door that he just came out of and push it back open, making my way back inside the hotel.

I quickly walk through the kitchen and nobody seems to notice me; I guess I fit in better back here with all the other waiters and waitresses. I shove my briefcase and coat under a table that has a long tablecloth and pick up a tray of water glasses.

Re-entering the Hedge Fund forum through the kitchen, I shield my face with the tray, and move towards Benson, who's now seated at a table.

"There's lot of anger and denial about what's going on right now. It's important to remember, it's not human nature that changes. Fear and greed are always the two drivers of the market. Now excuse me gentlemen, I won't be staying for lunch."

Surrounded by guards, Benson rises, and starts to leave the Forum.

I hurry behind him, putting the tray down, remembering to grab my briefcase and coat on my way out.

They move into a private stairwell and rush down the stairs. I follow and one of Benson's guards, thinking he heard something, stops.

I don't move.

Realizing he heard nothing, he starts moving again with the group. They exit through the rear door of the hotel, and enter two waiting black Lincoln town cars. I watch as the town cars drive off.

Realizing Benson's escaping me, I run around the corner and hail a taxi. One pulls over, and I jump in, "Follow those town cars!"

The cab speeds across town and I lean forward to better watch from the backseat. "Don't lose them!"

The cab driver nods. He darts in and out of lanes keeping close behind. They're probably just taking Benson back to his office, I realize. Benson will step out of the car, I'll catch up to him, and I'll try to get some time with him.

All I need are a few minutes.

All I need is a chance.

"You're doing great," I tell the driver, realizing how I'd love for somebody to say those three little words to me right now.

He nods.

We start going down Second Avenue and then turn into the Queens

Midtown Tunnel. I look around, dumbstruck.

"Looks like they're leaving the city," he says."Do you want me to keep going? This is going to cost you."

"Where do you think they're going?" I ask, as if the driver has any idea. I'm desperate and I'm sick and tired of being in this desperate state.

It seems to be a *perpetual state.*

Stop trading and all your problems will cease, a little voice tells me. But I drown it out. "Just keep following!"

Thirty minutes pass, and we're now speeding down the Long Island Expressway. The meter reads $144.83 and we start pulling into JFK Airport.

At an intersection, one of the black town cars goes left and the other goes right.

"Which one do you want me to follow?" the driver asks calmly, but I am anything but calm at this point.

I did not see which car Benson got into, and it never occurred to me that the cars would separate. "I don't know," I stammer.

The driver goes left. "Fifty percent odds I picked correctly."

"Those are good odds," I reply, feeling hopeful. "Really good odds," I add, knowing once again I'm probably deluding myself.

The black town car winds its way along the perimeter road, past commercial airliners, and then takes the first right off an exit ramp.

We're now all driving onto the aviation airfield. "Looks like somebody's boarding a private jet," the cab driver says.

An Airbus A340-300 with its engines running, idles at the end of the taxiway.

The town car stops in front of it, and men get out, passing a stewardess and a mechanic to the stairs of the plane. They board. The stewardess turns and follows them inside.

The cab driver pulls over beside the jet.

I realize I'm too far in this now to turn around and go back. I hand the driver three crisp one hundred dollar bills, and say, "Thank you."

I race up to the plane toward the mechanic.

"Are you the stewardess?" he asks, reminding me that I'm still wearing the waiter vest.

"I am, yes, but the proper term for it is 'air-hostess.' In the aviation industry, the term steward is almost obsolete, so please remember going forward that 'air hostess,' is more internationally accepted and most commonly used for gender neutrals and it's in accordance with our duties as cabin crew."

I rush onto the plane before he even has a chance to register what I just said.

Looking around, I seem to be invisible. I don't even see Benson on the flight.

I take the first empty seat that I see, and put on a pair of eye covers to shield my face. The doors to the plane close, and we take off.

I pretend to be asleep for the rest of the flight to – *wherever.*

24

Chapter 24

We're on our second leg of this journey and I started getting friendly with some of the passengers. We're riding on a small seaplane now, and although I'm no longer wearing the waiter's vest, I still have no idea where it is that we're going.

"I know what you mean," I say, chewing on some warm nuts and drinking a cold glass of Pellegrino. "This is my first episode with Benson," I reveal, having no idea what I'm talking about. "How about you?"

"No, we've been to Benson's private island many times."

Ahhh, his private island.

I observe one of the distinguished men sitting across from me. He's eating a slice of decadent red velvet cake. The cake lies on a china plate and he keeps pressing the "service" button.

He looks agitated and when the stewardess arrives, she asks, "Yes?" in her most helpful voice.

"I need some Diet Coke asap!"

"I'm sorry, sir, we're out of Diet Coke. Can I get you a regular Coke or something else?"

"Wait a minute! You're out of Diet Coke?!" he splutters, raising his voice.

She nods. "I'm very sorry."

He takes another bite of his decadent, probably nine thousand calorie piece of red velvet cake, and gasps, "That's outrageous."

"Again, I am so sorry. How can I help?" She's so apologetic you'd think she just blew off his arm with a grenade.

He shoos her off with the wave of his hand. "Can you believe this? Out of Diet Coke?" he asks to anyone who will listen.

He won't let it go and I'm about to say something rude, but instead I change the subject since the vibe on the plane has now turned toxic. "So how many people are expected at this soiree? I can hardly wait to arrive."

"It's hardly a soiree," a bald man replies. "He's hosting a Climate Change Summit."

I think about this. "Oh, I see."

The irony.

"So we're flying on a private jet to a climate change summit?" I ask. "Is this plane electric?"

Everyone looks at each other, unsure of how to respond.

"Hypocrisy is a pillar for the global warming sect," the disgruntled man, sans the Diet Coke, states.

I nod, wiping the salt from the nuts off of my lips with a napkin. "Well, I bet the food's outstanding."

"Steak I hear," someone else quips.

"By the time we get there, it'll be time for my nap," another divulges.

"Benson was early on Bitcoin," another remarks, "hence his 'private island' (air quotes) but his intentions are good though."

"I'm sure they are," I reply, smiling. "I see we're riding on the winds of change."

Leaning back in my leather seat, I turn toward the window, popping more nuts into my mouth, and realize that I can't even afford an Uber.

The seaplane swoops lower and finally signs of land appear. Miles of pristine white sandy beaches, aquamarine lagoons, and towering wooded cliffs come into view.

There's shady coconut palms, a rocky beach, and beyond that, buildings are cunningly carved into the wooded hillside. There's the main house, the guest house, pool building, reception hall...

We land, and motorcades line up and whisk us off.

We pull into a massive compound, and a discreet guard in a blue cardigan waves us in, as iron gates swing open.

I look around, and never in my life have I seen anything more beautiful.

25

Chapter 25

After getting over the lavishness of the island, I quickly start to feel out of place. Men are standing in small groups, talking, and I'm all alone walking around. I look like a lone wolf.

If I thought the feeling at the Waldorf was bad, this is a thousand times worse.

I make my way over to the hired help. "Hi," I say, acting as if I am in full control of this situation, "I'm here for my meeting with Steven Benson."

A young island girl wearing a Hawaiian shirt and shorts, asks, "Is he expecting you?"

"Yes," I say, smiling.

She stands in front of a computer screen behind a large mahogany desk and types something in. I stand there waiting, looking around.

As she watches me, I smile wider. "The name is Jolette Marco," I reveal, as if that name should have any clout, as if I'm somebody important and not some hanger-on who just jacked myself onto a plane, and crashed an island party.

"I'm so sorry, Ms. Marco, I'm not showing your appointment on my calendar. Are you here for the VIP lunch? Because that already started."

"I am, yes. My flight just got in. Apologies for my tardiness."

"Okay, let me have Juan escort you down there."

Seconds later, "Juan," is barreling around the corner in a golf cart waving at us. He rings his little bell. "Ms. Marco, oh, Ms. Marco, over here!"

He's smiling as if I just handed him a million dollars.

"Perfect," I say, "Thank you so much."

I hop on the golf cart with Juan and he starts speeding through the narrow dirt roads of the island.

"What a beautiful day," I say, trying to make small talk, kind of enjoying the ride. He nods. I don't think he understands any English other than my name. He looks at me and keeps smiling as he drives.

We hit a bump in the road and I almost fall off the cart. I start laughing and hold on tight to the pole above us. Juan takes another curve really fast… "Whoa," I tell him, but I'm loving the speed nonetheless.

After twenty minutes of this, we finally make it over to the other side of the island. Juan stops in front of a large glass building that's four stories high. He doesn't say anything and he's still smiling.

I thank him, get off the cart, and head for the building. Inside, I face more guards, and say in my sweetest voice, "Hi, I'm here for the VIP luncheon."

One waves for me to follow and we walk down a long, sterile corridor. Approaching a large glass door, he opens it, and I step into a beautiful room where there are white roses everywhere. It looks like a scene of a wedding. It the center of the room, ten men are seated. Everybody turns and looks at me.

I move toward Benson's table and my heart is racing.

"But if you own good stocks in good companies, you'll be fine."

I torpedo down into the middle of their conversation. "Like

Sequenom."

Benson looks up. "Now there's a name I'm familiar with."

"Based on last year's earnings consensus, the company has an estimated P/E ratio of 9, which is well below its projected earnings growth of 28%" I say, shifting the figures. "We've taken a closer look at the stock and —"

"—How did you get past my guards?"

"What guards?" I ask in my most serious voice. "I was honored when we received the invitation and I made it a priority to be here."

I hope to throw him off by the "we." If push comes to shove, I'll drop Monique's name. Although being that I'm not even allowed anywhere near the Benson files or even the filing *cabinet for that matter*, I'm not sure how crashing his island party will go over. Oh, wait, sorry: "The Climate Change Summit."

"We being?" Benson questions.

"ABLX Securities," I admit, backed against a wall.

"You're one of Monique's girls, I expect."

I nod. "I don't like to be thought of as one of Monique's or as a girl, but yes, I guess."

He stares at me intently. "May I see your card?"

I remove an expensive card holder and extract a card. Benson smiles, soothingly, "Come, sit."

The men part ways for me, and a nearby waiter sets up an extra chair.

Benson waits politely until I'm settled and then he glances at the card. "Jolette Marco,' I believe I know your brother..."

"—I'd appreciate it if you'd decide for yourself whether or not I'm qualified to —"

A waiter puts down a colossal steak in front of Benson. He ignores the dish and cuts me off, "Did Monique send you?"

"No. I came because I want you to look at this."

I take out Rick's file and hand it to him.

Benson glances at it, turning a page or two. "You think you can concatenate the stock with this? I know your brother. And I bet I know you too. You worked with him but you wanted out of that life, so you took off, quit grad school, you'll make it on your own, without big brother… That attitude got you all the way to A B L X…"

His every word strikes me like a tiny, precise jab.

But I clench my teeth, won't give ground. "Brave analysis, Mr. Benson. But are you confident enough to take Sequenom up a few notches to where it really belongs? Or maybe you just don't see it."

For an instant, his face opens with insecurity. But he returns to his sycophants and becomes as still and remote as a statue.

Frustrated, I pick up my briefcase and go, leaving the reports on the table.

26

Chapter 26

Heading out to the beach, I flop down into the sand. I take off my blouse and skirt and use it as a makeshift towel and stare out into the water. This place is so remote and exclusive, I lean back and let the hot sun beam all over my body.

It's instant relief.

The ocean looks beautiful. The water is like oil, so calm and peaceful, and I strip down naked and decide to go swimming. I swim for what seems like hours, burning off all my tension.

When I get out of the water, I lay on my clothes probably ruining them, *but what will it matter anyway?*

I just blew this whole thing.

I'm sure Monique will hear about it and I won't have a job to return to anyway. Maybe that wouldn't be such a bad thing.

No. This is bad.

I needed Benson and I blew it.

"What's up?" Noel asks on the first ring when I call him. I'm surprised I even have cell service.

"Benson didn't buy in," I say, cutting right to the chase.

"What?"

"You heard me. He doesn't want any part of it… He…"

I hear a police siren in the background. "You gave him the reports?!" Noel asks when they pass.

"Yes, I gave him the reports."

I can picture Noel brushing his hand through his blonde hair distractedly, the way he usually does when he gets nervous or upset. "What happened with the car?" I ask. "Are the police looking into it?"

"Yeah, yeah," he says, dismissing it. "Don't worry about it. Go back to the hotel, I'll call and tell you what to do," he says and clicks off, barely able to contain his annoyance.

I sit there and think for a moment that maybe its better that Benson does not take part in this scheme, that this all ends, right here, right now.

But I don't want to let Noel down.

And I can't let my father down.

I have to find another way.

I remember that I have Benson's cell phone number memorized, and I dial it.

I'm surprised when he answers. "Mr. Benson, it's Jolette Marco calling," I say jovially. "I have some excellent news. Sequenom is about to obtain approval for their P21 Down Syndrome test. Do you have any idea what that market potential is? You'll easily make 30% on your money if you get in now."

"Jolette, I appreciate your moxie, but I have a broker already at ABLX."

"I understand, Mr. Benson, but we can still open a separate account," I counter, "a DBA. All I would need is a different tax ID number."

I wait for his reaction.

If I have not learned how to manipulate paperwork at ABLX Securities… then I have learned nothing at all from Monique.

"My island office. 6:00 p.m. I'll listen."

"Thank you, sir!" I punch my fist in the air, elated!

* * *

As I make my way back to the main back building, a bunch of teenage girls run past me toward the water. They're escorted by older men, security guards, I imagine.

"What are you doing here?" one of the men asks.

"Swimming," I say, stating the obvious. "What's with the girls?"

They don't answer. I keep moving, and arrive to the main building and I'm relieved to see Juan standing at the front desk with the other guards.

"Hello Ms, Marco, are you ready to sit in on the Climate Change Summit now?"

"I need to get back my suite first, but I seem to have left my key back at the check in."

"Are you in the A block or B?"

Having no idea what he's talking about, I pretend I do. *I mean, why stop now?* "A."

He leads me over to his golf cart. "I have extra keys, come on, I'll take you."

After another joy ride with Juan where I almost lose my life, he finds a large available suite for me and opens the door. "At your service, Ms. Beautiful Marco," he says, handing me the key.

I thank him, double bolt the door when he leaves, and collapse down on the bed.

I have one hour to prepare myself.

I must sell Benson.

27

Chapter 27

Waiting in an icy conference room for ninety minutes before I get to see Steve Benson, I'm climbing the walls. His island offices are vast and square in their dimensions and a vaulted ceiling appears to float up into infinity. A gigantic crystal chandelier drops in the center of the room and it's surrounded by a floor-to-ceiling-length fish tank.

I call my brother to find out how things are going. "Hi Troy, how's the cat?"

"The cat's okay," he mutters. "When are you coming home? He keeps meowing and stuff. I don't like it."

"I'll be home Friday. Why is the cat meowing?"

"I don't know! What do I look like, a doctor? He meows and walks around a lot, that's it."

"Does he have his food and water?"

"Yes."

"How's work? Did you manage to get any?" I ask.

"I'm not working, Jolette. I have other problems I'm dealing with."

"It helps Troy, to be in a routine, keep your mind busy, stay focused, get a nice job."

"Oh, listen to you, Miss Corporate America. Nobody hates jobs more than you do, so save the rap!"

I change the subject. "How's Dad?"

"Yeah, he's here."

"He's there?" I ask, alarm bells going off.

"Yeah, you wanna talk to him?"

"Sure."

My father gets on the line. "Hello, Jolette. Hang on one second."

"Sure, Dad."

I wait. It sounds like he's moving into the bathroom or something. I hear a door close. "Jolette, are you there?"

"Yes, Dad."

"I … they called Sarah about your brother last night… from a bar. She had to go over and get him."

Oh, great.

I act surprised, but this comes as no surprise.

"Something needs to be done, Jolette. He's getting really bad and… I'm worried."

"I know Dad, I have it all figured out. I'm working really hard. I'm going to pay you back, and then I'm going to make some extra money. When that happens, we can put him in one of those rehab programs. Okay?"

The receptionist is waving to me that it's time.

"Okay, Dad? I have to go now, all right? I'll see you soon."

I click "end call," as the receptionist knocks and opens the conference room door. "They're ready for you now, Ms. Marco."

"Thank you."

"May I get you something to drink?" she offers. "We have fresh juice."

"No thank you," I reply, trying to shrug off that conversation that I just had with my father.

I glide into the conference room with my head held high, rigid determination set in my shoulders.

Steve Benson and his team of money managers sit back like the Gods of Olympus.

The twelve well dressed tycoons wield immense international influence and their combined wealth easily adds up to hundreds of billions of dollars.

I take out my reports and pass them around. On the table are stacks of documents, the word "CONFIDENTIAL" prominent on many of the folders. My eyes gaze upon the exorbitant art that's showcased around the room.

I try to breathe evenly, try to remain calm, as I begin my presentation.

Twenty minutes into it, they're shaking their heads in disagreement. "The balance sheet of this company isn't sound," one says. "You're asking for a large equity position, and under the current market environment, these numbers are just terrible."

Another investor adds, "The P/E ratios are disturbing."

I rivet my eyes on them one by one as another potential investor speaks, "Sequenom has always been a risky play…"

This can't be happening!

My anxiety accelerates. Pain in my chest become razor sharp. "Look," I say, raising my voice. "This is a no-brainer. No one has ever lost money backing us."

"Not yet. But biotechs are a new endeavor for you," Benson states. His tone is snappish, impatient.

I take a sip of water, very aware of his close scrutiny. I adopt a ruthless manner, one I never even knew I possessed until now. "Cambridge and Levanthal are taking down 39.3 million shares. We're talking leverage. It's a win, win."

They look at each other.

And then I decide to lie. It's the only way to navigate through these complicated shark infested waters. "And Warren's coming in for fifty million."

"Buffet's in?" they ask incredulously.

It was said so coolly and with such confidence, they believe me.

"I can secure the other half with my own accounts," I add, adroitly throwing the ball back at them.

The money managers stare at me, speechless. Benson's glance is approving.

"Well. It's late. I expect an answer by the morning," I conclude, as Benson follows me out of the conference room.

I turn to him, all business. "Prepare the SEC filing papers and have them ready. I'll tell you when to pull the trigger."

He shepherds me toward the elevator, "You're very good at giving orders, Jolette. Maybe you should consider working for me someday."

I look at him with a small, challenging smile. "Great idea, Mr. Benson. Perhaps someday. That would be an honor."

He presses the elevator button. "You can count me in for two million shares," he announces, a tremulous smile spreading across his face.

"Well, that's fantastic, sir, but I was hoping you'd come in for ten."

"Ten million, Jolette? Really?"

I nod.

"How about eight?" he counters.

"Eight million works," I agree, and shake his hand.

The elevator doors open and I get in, and when those doors close, my eyes turn as cold as stone.

28

Chapter 28

"He took it, he's in," I tell Noel over Skype.

I get out of the shower, my hair is dripping wet, and I stare at him over Skype.

He's sitting in front of his ten monitors at home. "For how much?"

"Eight million."

"Wow! Eight million!" He punches some figures into his computer. "Nice work, Jolette, you scored!"

I stand in my underwear and a thick, white towel that's just covering my breasts, brushing my wet, long hair. I must have gotten some sun today because my cheeks are flush.

Or maybe it's just because I'm talking to Noel.

I get under the warm bed sheets and I don't plan to move for the next twelve hours.

"When's this going down?" I ask.

"Tomorrow."

"Tomorrow?" I gasp, sitting up.

"Yep. Sequenom needs to hit 90. This thing is a ticking time bomb."

I wasn't planning on getting back to San Francisco until the day after tomorrow, and I still have to collect my suitcase at the Four Seasons.

I jump out of bed and start to get dressed, pulling out my laptop so I can purchase a ticket for a red eye flight home tonight. I'm not going to miss out on this action. I had to be back on that trading floor.

I start to get dressed and walking around in my pink and black eyelet underwear, I'm unaware that Noel is still watching me. I put my pearls back on and my white blouse. "Are we going to chill?" I hear Noel ask, "When you get home?"

I'm rushing around trying to find my skirt. "Chill?" I ask, turning back to him.

He nods.

"I don't chill, Noel, that's how you end up with children."

He laughs. He looks so jolly and happy when he laughs.

And I laugh too. It's the first time I've laughed in months.

It feels good.

I feel good.

Sequenom is going to climb, and my life is about to get much better.

My cell phone is about to die, and I have plans to make. "I have to go, Noel," I say, looking back at his face one final time over Skype. "I'll see you back in San Francisco."

29

Chapter 29

Wild Juan wanted to take me back to the airport, but I managed to get a real car and a real driver. When I exit the car in the pitch dark on the landing field, I thank the driver and board the seaplane.

There's only one other passenger on the flight and he reaches out to shake my hand, "Hi, I'm Daniel Lutz. Nice to meet you." He has his laptop open in front of him.

"Jolette Marco," I reply, taking the business card that he hands me. Once I'm settled in my seat, I reach into my briefcase, and hand him mine.

He glances at it. "ABLX Securities? We don't invite brokers to our Climate Change Summits," he says, looking back at me with a suspicious look.

I glance down at his card to see what I'm dealing with here: Daniel Lutz, Vice President, Operations, Benson LLC.

Great, a Benson employee.

And there's something off about him. He has an edginess. A nervousness. He turns back to his laptop, shaking his head, and ignores me for the rest of the flight.

"Climate Change is my jam," is all I say.

There are two sides in this business; the buy side and the sell side. The sell side is the glorious side that I'm on. Where we kiss ass to the clients; the institutional investors, the hedge funds.

They're the privileged set; the buy side. And even though you may make bank for what you do and maybe you even have your own status and prestige on Wall Street, you just aren't one of *them.*

Every guy on the sell side wants to make it over to the buy side someday. It's a leap. And it's what everybody wants.

Some people get it. Most don't.

As for me... after losing all of my father's money, I don't think I'd ever want to manage somebody else's money again.

* * *

Four hours later, I'm moving through a bustling JFK airport, and it's a complete shift from being away on that remote, private island.

I managed to call the Four Seasons, and I checked out over the phone. I asked if they could ship my bag for me, and they said yes, which saved me a trip back into the city.

With the extra time, I head into the gift shop so I can buy some souvenirs for Devin and Dan. I pick out two I LOVE NEW YORK T-shirts and a Statue of Liberty figurine.

After I wait in the long line to pay, I realize I have enough money leftover for dinner, and I make my way over to the first restaurant I see.

It's crowded so I take a seat at the bar.

A waitress comes over with a pot of coffee. She pulls a mug out in front of me. "Coffee, dear?"

"Yes, please, thank you."

"You know what ya want?" she asks in a strong NYC accent. I open the menu and I only have twenty dollars left. I want to be able to leave her a decent tip. "I'll take the grilled chicken sandwich."

"Ya want fries with it?"

I'm not sure how much the fries will cost and I can't find the price on the menu. I look up at her. "Do they come with it?" I ask humbly.

"Three dollars extra," she responds hurriedly, looking around.

"Yes, that would be great. Thank you." She walks off and I take six packets of sugar and dump them into my coffee.

Scrimping and saving so much of my money so I can use it for trading, I rarely have any leftover for the small luxuries like affording sugar at home for my coffee.

I take a sip and it's sweet and delicious!

Oh, the simple pleasures!

My chicken sandwich arrives and I dig in, pouring ketchup all over the chicken and fries. I study stock charts from my phone while I eat. I have food. I'm alone. And I'm about to make radical money.

JACKPOT!

A man sits down at the end of the bar beside me. He puts his phone and a copy of the NY Post down near me. He's in the end seat so we face each other like in an L shape.

I can feel him watching me, and uncomfortable, I remove some paper and a pen from my purse, and I start to make a to-do list:

1. Tonight: fly home.
2. Tomorrow morning: Go straight into work. After, pick up Sam at Troy's.
3. Saturday: go into work to handle paperwork
4. Sunday: see family
5. Soon: Amass 1 million dollars, quit ABLX Securities.

I put my pen down, happy with this plan.

I look up and the man is still staring at me. He's in his mid-thirties with dark hair and blue eyes and he looks like John Hamm, the actor. He's very good looking.

I focus back on my stock charts; I've had enough small talk over this past week and I'm hoping he doesn't start in, but he does. "Writing your obituary?" he asks.

"What?" I reply, taken aback.

"Your obit?" he repeats ominously. "Whatever you're writing, you seem very intense."

"Oh, it's just my game plan."

"Okay," he says, and then he shoves his NY Post in front of me. "She really took him to the cleaners."

Staring back at me on Page Six is a large photo of a reality TV star and a story about how she hoodwinked her poor eighty year old husband, a lawyer, for his money.

I turn away, looking for the waitress so I can get my bill and make my flight, but he keeps waving his newspaper underneath me. "You see," he says, low voiced, "She thought she had her ticket to ride…"

Unable to avoid him any longer, I say, "Her ticket to ride? He cheated on her and now she's taking the fall as the bad guy for leaving him."

"Ahh, so it's not always as it seems, is it?"

His words linger in the air.

"No. It's not," I reply, as a cold shiver runs through me.

"In the end, everybody gets what they deserve, don't they?" he adds, and then he hands me his business card. "If you ever want to talk, call me."

When he leaves, I glance down at his card: "Cullen Steele, FBI, Department of Investigations, Crime Unit."

I start shaking and drop the card down on the counter. The waitress walks by me saying, "Hun, pay up at the front."

I realize that the bill was sitting under my glass of water the whole time. "Don't forget ... you're gonna pay..." she adds.

I look back up at her.

"You're gonna pay..." she repeats, but walks off before she even finishes her sentence.

30

Chapter 30

7:00 a.m. I enter the ABLX Securities lobby in the same clothes that I've been in for the past forty-eight hours, and rifle through the Wall Street Journal that I just bought from the building newsstand. I find the article that I'm looking for: Sequenom Exonerated In Biotech Marketing Malpractice.

I smack my hands in the air, and bound the elevator, victorious!

* * *

Sequenom trades higher for most of the morning, and then I get a text from Noel. "Keep your eyes peeled to the screens. The news is going to hit at noon."

I keep looking at the TV monitors hanging from the ceilings. They are closed captioned along the bottoms of the screens, and a female reporter begins to read the mid-day news.

I'm silent, an absorbed look on my face, as I dial in an order: "Buying 450,000 SQN 56 for Bernstein Capital."

I dial another client, "Sequenom's in play. Everyone's a buyer."

And then it's time...

At noon, I bow my head and wait. With my hands cupped in my lap, I close my eyes.

The trading floor goes very quiet. The PR release comes over the wires and then the trading floor erupts – howling and screaming! This place turns loud and aggressive!

I jump out of my chair and pick up another ringing phone! "Sequenom just landed two new contracts! Stock popped another fourteen points!"

I reach for my cell phone and read Noel's text: "You see it?!"

"I see it!"

Raising my eyes, I take in the scene on the trading floor at a glance. The feeling of being on the right sight of the trade, the feeling of making this much money … is incredible.

By the end of the day, Sequenom closed up 75%.

By my calculations, I had the first half of my father's money back.

Not bad for a fast week of work.

Not good for someone who is already down another $198,000.

Yet every account…

Ticket clocked.

Trade executed.

Commission racked.

Profit made.

Priceless.

* * *

I head down to the compliance office after the market closes and I approach the cage, looking around for Jesus. He's sitting by a dead plant.

My steely gaze is enough to jar him out of his workday boredom. "Hi Hey-Zeus, how's it going? The system isn't allocating me these account numbers. Can you help?"

I bend forward, handing him a file.

"This is a Benson account," Jesus announces. "Monique will have to sign off on this."

My eyes widen. "That won't happen today, Jesus," I respond. "I've got about 80 million dollars worth of trades I need to book tonight."

"We'll, let's try and get her on the phone then," Jesus says and picks up the phone. He looks over the trade tickets impressed. "Sequenom. Looks like you hit the winning numbers today."

I glance at the clock. I am not somebody who flusters easily, but I'm getting there now.

"She's not on the floor. Let me try her cell."

"Stop, Jesus!" I look around. "Look. We don't need to call Monique. Do you have a personal account here at the firm?"

He nods.

I lower my voice. "I'll float you three hundred shares."

Jesus smiles. "Done. And done."

31

Chapter 31

At 1:15 p.m. that afternoon, Troy picks me up at work with Sam in his cat carrier in the backseat of his car, and he looks worse for wear.

I'm grateful to see my brother, but more so my cat, and I take the carrier from the backseat and put it on my lap. I start to pet my babe. "Hi Sammy, how's my little lover boy? I missed you so much. Yes, I did, yes, I did…" He hears my voice and I know he's content, and now I feel content.

I turn to my brother, "Dad's worried about you, Troy."

"Oh, really? Well not as worried as he is about you."

I shake my head, "Troy, I'm on a roll…"

"Oh, yeah?! Another roll?! Until you blow up again? How long will it take this time?"

"How many beers did you have when Sarah picked you up the other night?"

"Oh, please. You lie about your losses the same way I lie about my drinking. But your lying is worse. You know why, Jolette? Because you are affecting *everyone.* Dad needed that money – but you had to take it and run it into the ground.

He's so dramatic.

I can't wait to get home. "You need to check your attitude, Troy. Losses are a part of life."

"It's the story of your life, Jolette... the story of *your life...*" his voice trails off.

We don't talk for the rest of the ride which thankfully isn't long. When he pulls up in front of my apartment, I'm overtired and in dire need of a hot shower. "Thank you, Troy," I say, carefully carrying my cat and all his stuff, out of the car. "And thanks for watching him while I was gone."

I don't look at him.

I can't.

I don't want him to see this lingering fear in my eyes.

* * *

Entering my studio apartment after having been gone for four days, it's dark and cold and has a musty odor. I open some windows even though a few are already open, and when I turn the lights on, my apartment looks like a rat's hole.

I have to move, I remind myself.

It's a rent-controlled deal and I moved in six years ago, but the paint is starting to peel and the rug is a filthy brown, and though I've never complained before, after staying at the Four Seasons and the resort on the Benson's island, this place is just dismal with a capital D.

I set up Sam's food, water, and his litterbox, and then I take a long hot shower.

When I get out, I flop on my couch in my clean underwear, sweatpants and a sweatshirt. I'm warm and cozy and wrap warm blankets on top of me. I have a frozen pizza baking in the oven, and when I pour myself some Diet Coke, I smile, remembering that man on the plane.

Turning on the TV, I turn out the lights and watch some reality shows so I can zone out.

But an hour in and halfway through my pizza, I start to get antsy. I reach for my iPad and start studying stock charts. All the indexes are at all time highs but the small cap names are getting pulverized. Crypto, the miners, the pot stocks, the meme stocks are all at all-time lows.

The manipulation is insane.

So many bag holders.

I take a closer look at Sequenom and the three-day chart looks rancid. Every green candle has been whacked down, followed by a large red one. It seems that every time the stock wanted to move higher, somebody was on the other side hammering it.

I get a sickening feeling.

I feel like this whole thing is a house of cards. I needed to get to Rick and find out how long it's going to take to get my money. I needed to pay my father back. I need to be done with this.

I get off the couch, throw on some jeans, and decide to pay Rick a visit.

32

Chapter 32

I approach the indiscreet four story walk-up, and Dominic, the security guard, is just leaving the building. We pass each other on the street, but don't say "hello."

"What are you here for?" a different security guard asks when I walk up the steps. "There's no meeting today."

"I'm here to see Rick. Is he here?"

"No meeting today," he repeats.

"I need to see Rick. Do I stutter?"

The guard's eyes penetrate mine. "Follow me."

We walk inside and go upstairs, and he opens a sliding bullet proof door that's at the end of the hallway.

Rick is seated and monitoring over one hundred trading systems. "What is it, Marco?" he asks impatiently.

"Where's my money?"

"What are you talking about, Jolette? The money will be wired. You need to give it some time."

"How much time?"

"The accounts in Switzerland take longer to process. And remember, you're not the only lieutenant we have working here. There are over one hundred Jolette Marco's. So watch your step."

"No, you watch your step, Rick. I control Benson – remember that."

"Whoever has the leverage has the power, and we have that power – The Triad. We can always get someone else to pull Benson's strings."

"Is that right, Rick?"

"That's right," he says, giving me a look that could kill.

I walk around and stare at the hundreds of mainframes. "What's this?" I ask, pointing to one of the larger systems.

"That's electromagnetic radiation. It operates in a 1.0GHz to 30GHz spectrum and a good signal can travel as much as 300 kilometers or around 186 miles," he says.

"So our orders go off first?"

He nods.

"Always good to be reassured that the market reflects intrinsic value instead of behaving like a high tech casino."

"It would be a casino if it depended on random factors in which case no information or speed would be needed. We profit from economy of scale, Jolette. Those who want profits, must invest."

Rick circles me and keeps talking, "Let's say you, as a retail investor, wanted to buy stock in ...Amazon. Your order will be filled at or near the prevailing market price by your brokerage house. The bid and ask quotes are always to the penny, but the prices of executed trades can be carried out to three, four, or even six decimal places. No sane human trader would spend their time haggling over a ten-thousandth of a cent."

"No, but your computers don't get bored, do they?"

"They don't. And here's where the dangerous part sets in. It's not that traders are less involved, it's that they can't be involved. By the time an ordinary investor sees a quote, it's like looking at a star that burned out thousands of years ago. Ninety percent of quotes are canceled before execution, and most aren't even real; they're just there to test the market — to confuse or subvert competing algorithms."

"So why do we even have stock markets, Rick, huh?"

"To promote business investment, that's the textbook answer, and the guarantee of liquidity."

"But if these trading systems are canceling more than 90% of their orders, then when a mutual fund has a big position to move, they pay more for stocks they're buying, and less for stock's they're selling. That money is ultimately taken out of the hands of the long-term investor."

"That's right. You see these systems here? They track and trade on those moves."

"Trading ahead? Front running?" I ask, already knowing the answer.

"Yep."

As I become more aware of the large motorized sound of these machines, it begins to rattle my brain. And as I try to grasp the enormity of this, I want to escape. I'm starting to wonder at this point, if there's *any escape ever*. Because when Rick's paycheck arrives, I know I'll be holding paradise in my hands.

Yet I worry when does seven figures become the new six figures?

This Society, in spite of its anonymity and secrecy, fills me with a peculiar terror. There's something oppressive about Rick and the other money managers, and even Noel, and how they operate. It's a place of hushed silences, seclusion and hidden mysteries. And I want this to end: this noise, this predicament, this life.

"Do the math, Jolette. We reap *billions.* Six and a half billion, to be exact last quarter..."

"No one has a legitimate shot at getting a fair deal. The markets have lost their integrity, and I think I've heard enough. I have to go."

"One more thing, Jolette."

I look back at him. He hits a button on his remote and up on the screen a large chart appears. A jagged line with a V like plunge follows a large vertical leap up. "That was the flash crash. You remember that day, don't you?"

Of course I remember that day. The Dow dropped 1,000 points in minutes.

"Be careful, it can very well happen again."

"Rick, when one of your rogue algorithms goes into an infinite loop and cannot stop, you will throw Wall Street into another tailspin and the entire global economy off kilter."

"That's right. And the pieces are already in place. So be careful. You wouldn't want to be on the wrong side of it."

It's a lethal weapon. "May I go now, Rick?" I ask. I wait for him to open the door.

He presses a button behind his desk, and the large heavy door slowly slides open.

I exit, shaken.

Walking down the dark hallway, I see…

It can't be.

It is.

Noel is coming toward me.

What's he doing here?

That's exactly what he asks me. "What are you doing here?"

"I had to talk to Rick. You?"

His intelligent eyes narrow. "Same here." He wraps his arms around my waist and pulls me toward him. "I'm on my way to AdventureWorld," he whispers in my ear. "Little meeting with the CEO, care to join me? It'll be a date."

I don't say anything. "Come on, don't you like rollercoasters?" he asks, giving me his killer grin. "I get the private VIP tour."

I melt. Besides, it does sound kind of fun.

Cinder block by cinder block, there's been a wall of safety that I've built around myself. I prefer to be insulated from life and I'd rather not trust anybody, including Noel. But right now, whether I wanted to or not, I couldn't help myself.

I smile, and then I nod.

"Go and wait outside for me. I just need to deal with Rick for five minutes, and then we'll take off."

Noel playfully smacks me on my backside and as I walk off, I can't wait.

33

Chapter 33

We arrive at AdventureWorld in under an hour. A black panther paces back and forth at the gate entrance. Beyond it is the Big Bear Rollercoaster — a seven-car train designed to sway side-to-side at a 110 degree angle.

Walking around, Noel and I gawk like school kids. The park is overpopulated with kids, overheated and screaming, chugging down sugary drinks and sweets of every kind.

There are a multitude of rides: wave pools, tiger acts, a 100 foot high erupting volcano, an indoor rainforest, a shark aquarium, a secret garden, a dolphin house, a white-tiger habitat.

And tons of animals!

The atmosphere is frivolous and Noel makes me laugh a great deal. We have our own VIP private tour guide, and he escorts us around the park. I pick at a complimentary box of animal cookies, as Noel blows soap bubbles. He looks debonair in a casual Prada sports jacket and perfectly pressed slacks.

Approaching the Big Bear Rollercoaster, we sweep past the long line and through the glaring green neon entrance that's disguised as a question mark and into the confines of The Riddler's lime-green industrial laboratory.

Once we're seated on the rollercoaster, Noel says with conviction. "Keep opening new accounts, and you'll be banking over a million dollars every quarter in no time."

We buckle ourselves in and traverse up a 263-foot elevation. Click, Click, Click, Click…

He turns to me, "The question is, can you handle it?"

"I can handle it."

The rollercoaster takes us higher and higher and at the top, a sign reads: "Do Not Stand Up. Keep Your Hands Inside The Car."

"Hang on," Noel says, smiling into my eyes, "It's gonna be a bumpy ride."

Excitement thunders through my body. The coaster teeters on the brink of falling down — and state-of-the-art electromagnetic motors blast the aerodynamic coaster.

It accelerates from zero to 100 mph in seven seconds! It then shoots straight up another 41-story tower!

We get whisked along the blazing red, orange and yellow twisted steel tracks encountering sudden plunges and huge sweeping spirals hands in the air, screaming and having the time of our lives!

* * *

"So… I've done my research and I've studied you. I know pretty much everything you do."

We're sitting at a casual, outdoor table eating hamburgers, and I want to get to know Noel better.

"You made your first million trading commodities. Then, gold, strategic metals for new tech, crypto, now the small cap sector."

"You said everything. Huh? Oh."

"…Can I ask you a personal question?"

"Sure."

"Why are you so into small cap stocks?" I ask him.

Noel ponders this for a moment. "Well, from a research standpoint, they're not stalwarts like large caps that can go up anytime. They need more attention and can only be bought by a certain type of individual."

Thoughtfully, he adds, "Only long-term investors can handle them, really. And once those stocks rise into their fullest potential, they generate the most awesome profit that's unreaped by the rest of the world. There's only those left on the sidelines, watching, as the rest of us cashed in."

I'm moved by his thoughtful response.

"I mean, large caps have momentum," he continues, "but they seem anti-climatic to me for some reason. I mean, by comparison. What about you? What got you into trading?"

"I guess it was initially through my brother. He had a big, kind of show-off portfolio. But then I found out that I had a really sharp mind for reading charts, and the more I studied, the more I liked what it made me think about."

"Oh yeah? Like what?"

"Like what a shyster he was."

Noel laughs, uncomfortably.

"But I do like to ponder the life of a stock. I like to weigh in on what was going on the year it hit its high. I wonder about all those people who held on and what did they do with their money. I love how stocks continue to transform, and how every time I look at one, it's going to be different than if I looked at it on any other day. Because it has a pulse, it's perpetually moving and changing until it tops, and then it begins its inevitable decline..."

Now Noel is blown away. "And that's when we go short..."

"That's right. Short. And ride it all the way down into the ground..."

Noel grins, "A billion here, a billion there... and pretty soon, we're talkin' real money."

We both laugh, soulmates at last.

* * *

Noel and I ride on a golf cart with our tour guide for fifteen minutes to the other side of the park, and approach the executive offices of AdventureWorld.

Noel thanks our guide, tips him heavily judging by the size of the guide's grin, and we make our way inside.

"What is this meeting?" I ask.

"Bryce Mallone, the CEO, is my client. This won't take long."

We enter the Executive Suites and Noel and I are escorted into Bryce's palatial office. Noel and Bryce shake hands. "We had a very nice time today, Bryce, thank you. That Big Bear rollercoaster is something else," Noel admires.

"Well, Noel, rollercoasters are fun to ride on, but you can't live on one," Bryce counters.

Noel nods, unsure, and then he turns to me."This is Jolette Marco, friend of mine."

Bryce shakes my hand. "Pleasure to meet you."

I notice some of the framed photographs of Bryce's family and it reminds me of Sarah's family and the coupons. "Oh, Bryce, by the way, the new coupon policy with the color coding... it's very confusing."

"Yeah, yeah, we had some problems with it," he dismisses.

"Yes, you know, my sister came all the way out here, and she was told the coupons were expired."

He shrugs it off. "Yeah, like I said, we've had some problems with it."

He can care less about it, and Noel shoots me a dirty look. "Bryce, we didn't talk about my fee, so I'll just dive right in."

"Let's finish this tomorrow, Noel. I have a lot on my plate."

Noel pulls out a laptop and looks increasingly nervous. "It won't take long."

"Noel, unfortunately, the Board's made some changes. They decided to go with Weisel instead of Rothman."

"What?!" Noel's voice rises. He grabs a chair, and steadies himself. "I made you fifty million last year and you let those "snakes" in the door?!"

"You know, Noel, I don't make the final decisions..."

"Who drove your stock price up when you were looking to liquidate your options? I DID!" Noel reminds him, throwing his hands in the air, anger rising. "And you sell me out, you bastard!"

"It's business, Noel."

Flushed and embarrassed, Noel exits.

I turn to Bryce, and then follow Noel out.

* * *

I walk behind Noel. We're both wearing sunglasses and there's screaming kids everywhere.

"This is just great," Noel stammers.

He keeps walking. Mind working. Tormented. "How are we going to spin this?"

"Forget it, Noel. It's spun."

He turns to me. "And what makes you think that, huh Jolette?! Wake up!" He gives me a look of utter coldness and disgust.

We walk to the VIP parking lot and I watch him in front of me, my heart pounding. I see Noel's expression as he walks; he's ready to explode.

"And you start discussing coupons?! I mean, Jolette, what the fuck is wrong with you!?"

"What do you mean?"

He starts mimicking me. "You know, Bryce, the new coupon policy with the color coding is confusing... Geesus!"

I can't believe the change in him. He gets even angrier.

"I'm trying to close business and you're standing there discussing COUPONS!"

"Oh, so now you have a problem with coupons?"

He just shakes his head, and keeps walking.

"You know what, Noel?! My nephews – sometimes the only time they get to go to the park is when my sister has some coupons! Okay?! Her husband is a math teacher. He doesn't make THE MONEY YOU MAKE! So get off your high horse!"

"My high horse, huh?!" He spins around, facing me. "My high horse put you where you are today!"

"You're so full of yourself, Noel," I say, shaking my head.

"Well, maybe that guy can teach you some math so you can finally learn how to trade."

I'm shocked. Now he's crossed the line.

I look up. To his eyes. Into them.

"There's a void in you that's so deep, Noel, every last penny in this world can't fill it."

I hit a chord. And then suddenly, he walks toward me like a violent gust of wind.

He stares at me. It's a loaded moment between us. And there's something in the way he looks at me...

He chokes, "I'm sorry." He reaches for me. "I'm so sorry, Jolette."

My eyes don't leave his face. They're bright with desire and expectation, and Noel brings my face towards his with his hands, and hooks his lips on mine, kissing me.

His fingers slide through my hair and he reaches around my waist, pulling me toward him.

He kisses me harder, it's as if all of his pain can diffuse if he breathes me in hard enough. I moan and breathe him in back, aching for him.

He masters my mouth with each touch of his tongue and I can't pull away… I'm entranced, losing myself in him, and a longing so deep within me awakens. It has been pushed down for so long that I'm achy, breathless, clinging to him, and I can't get enough of him.

34

Chapter 34

"Whoever makes it to the backyard first is the winner!!"

I race with my nephews on skateboards in Sausalito, and we're flying down the windy streets and even though they are little boys, I still need to win.

I was able to get some sleep over the weekend and feel rejuvenated. Noel has been in Dubai, and things were moving along. I still haven't been paid yet, but I know the money will hit, and everything will be back to normal again.

I barrel around a corner, bending my knees, now a half a block ahead of the twins and we're going down a hill... I take a corner fast, and Dan comes up close behind me; he's about to beat me, and I start laughing as he takes the lead, but at last minute, who's the winner — I am.

"Maybe next time, Dan," I say, laughing, jumping off the skateboard.

I take off my helmet because Sarah insists that we always wear one and I need to be a good influence on the twins, and I help them off with theirs. "You guys are getting good! Almost beat me! *Almost!*"

We go inside Sarah's house and she has tall glasses of lemonade waiting for us. My sister is such a good mother and so attentive. "Wash your hands," she tells the boys, "and get ready for lunch."

I move into the kitchen and my father is reading the San Francisco Chronicle. "Hi Dad."

With the money I paid him back so far, he's made some of the repairs on the boat and next week, he's moving back in. "How are you?"

He glances at me. "I'm well, Jolette, thank you."

There's still a tension between us. It's not as bad as it was, but it's still there. I sit down beside him with my lemonade. He already has a glass so I don't offer him any.

I open the bag of souvenirs that I bought for Devin and Dan which is sitting on the table. "I got these in New York."

"What were you doing in New York?" he asks.

"I was ... there for a work conference."

"Oh."

"Never in all my life have I seen a city as grand as that one, Dad. I mean, it has everything. The buildings are so high…and look, I took some photos of the hotel I stayed at and Central Park."

I open my phone to show my father the photos but he's not interested. "Troy says you're involved with some shady characters."

"What?! Oh, Dad, come on! As if Troy should talk!"

He nods, giving me a disappointed look. "That's what he told me."

"I'm working hard at my job, I made a lot of headway in New York. Bonuses are coming up at the end of the year, that should help out a lot financially…. Things are on the upswing."

"He tells me you may be involved in illegal activities."

"Illegal activities? What?! I would never do anything illegal!"

"Okay, no need to yell, Jolette."

I quiet myself.

"Jolette, you still have a lot to learn about human nature."

I drop my eyes. "I know, Dad."

"You don't want to go down the same road as your brother."

"No, Dad."

I watch my father and then squeeze his arm affectionately. To my surprise, he still pulls away.

And then he starts quoting the Bible. "What is it, Jolette, if you've gained the whole world but lost your soul?"

He gets up from the table and takes his glass of lemonade and puts it in the sink. "What, Dad?" I snap.

We glare at each other. "What did you say, Dad?" I repeat. My words come out cynical and sharp.

"Nothing."

The twins run into the kitchen wearing their new I LOVE NEW YORK T-shirts and they stand in front of me with a new deck of cards. "Aunt Jolette, can we show you our magic trick now?"

"Sure."

I shift my attention on the twins. "Let's see it," I say smiling.

Devin shuffles the cards, and they slide out of his hands and go everywhere."Ooops, I'm sorry..."

"No problem, Devin." I wait patiently as he gathers the cards, and starts the trick.

"Now where's your card?" he asks.

I always pick the right card. "It's right here; the eight of clubs."

Devin grins. "Are you sure, Aunt Jolette?"

"Of course I'm sure."

He reveals the card.

And I'm stunned to see the King of Hearts staring back at me.

He starts laughing. "You're wrong. Very wrong!" Devin rubs in.

"We tricked you, Aunt Jolette!!" Dan cackles, laughing along with his brother.

Devin adds, "Remember – nothing is at it seems."

I stare at them dumbfounded. *They tricked me.*

And suddenly a wave of paranoia runs through me. *And I have no idea where it stems from.*

35

Chapter 35

Sequenom has been trading all over the map. Rick still hasn't paid me, Noel has spent the last two weeks in Dubai and I haven't heard from him, and now we're sitting next to each other at our first Triad meeting in a while, and what really blows the top off of everything is when Rick says, "We're going in the other direction on Sequenom; it's now a short play."

I can't even believe the words.

"We moved the stock up twenty points and everybody should have made money. It's at a new weekly high, and it's time to ram it back down…" Rick continues. He stands at the podium and hundreds of heads nod in agreement.

"Ram it back down?!" I turn to Noel stunned.

He gives me a look to quiet down.

"Do you know how many clients I have in this right now?! Why didn't I get the fucking memo on this?"

"Jolette, keep your voice down."

But I'm so mad, I can feel my face turning red and people are staring at us. Noel turns away from me, and I grab his arm. "This can't be happening!"

"Shut. The. Fuck. Up," he says, with a look on his face like he's about to kill me.

Stunned, horrified, and feeling betrayed, I rise, and push my chair out from underneath me. I kick it and walk off.

Noel gets up and follows.

I feel like I'm going to lose my mind. I make my way for a staircase, any staircase. We're in another Society hell hole, some new basement because we are always switching locations, and I'm trying to find my way out... but I feel like a rat in a maze, trapped.

I can feel Noel gaining on me, and I start running up a rickety staircase. I get off at the next floor, trying to throw Noel off track, and I rush down a long wooden hallway that creaks with my every step. I push open a door that says, "Ladies Room."

It's old and smells like mothballs, and there are two stalls. I get into one and just as I'm about to slam the door, Noel is there and he pushes it open.

He stands in front of me. "What the hell just happened back there? You made a scene."

"I made a scene?! Why didn't you tell me about this?!"

"Tell you about what? We change directions on stocks, on currencies, on the value of NFT's all the time. So what's your problem?"

"I have clients in this, Noel! Clients who are going to get hammered! When is this news going to hit? How much time do I have?"

"It's happening right now, we are real time, and don't fall in love with a client, Jolette, that's the first rule of business."

"Oh, is it, Noel? Is that right? You know everything, don't you?"

He knows I'm hurt and betrayed, and there's not a thing he can do about it. So he defends himself. Like he always does. *As if what we're doing isn't wrong*. As if somebody else isn't getting the short end of the stick on this. Like I did once, like my father did once — in BED BATH AND BEYOND. The hell trade of a lifetime.

"You know what your problem is, Jolette? You don't see reality. You don't see the truth of what's right in front of you."

"Oh, fuck you, Noel, you don't have a clue as to what reality is."

I try to push past him away but he grabs my wrists.

"Let go of me," I say. My face is inches away from his. The pressure and tension with us is at an all time high.

"Or what?"

"Or you'll be sorry," I tell him, having no idea where that came from.

He's breathing heavy and I can see the veins in his forehead. He wants to say something but I'm not sure what, so I remain silent.

"You think..."

"I think what? Huh?" I ask seductively, almost whispering the words in his ear. His face now is so close to mine, and I can feel the warmth of his breath, his lips almost touch mine.

"I'm waiting, Noel." And I wonder if he has any idea right now how true the meaning of those words are. Because I am *waiting.* I have *been* waiting. So what the fuck, Noel?

Seriously what the fuck?

Naturally, I pull my shoulders back. I'm horny, I'm aroused, and I want him to take me right here in this bathroom and fuck me.

I wonder if he'd dare.

But what he says cuts right to the bone.

"You keep losing money because you keep buying premium. Because "the system" is rigged against you. Because these names, these shitty, beaten down names are all you can afford. Because the thrill of a quick hit satisfies your short term rush well before you're disciplined in a long term strategy that's finally going to pay off. One that will change your habits. Because you don't have a plan. Because you call this a hobby, not a business. Because you never really learned how to trade. Because you never acquired the capital or the knowledge to sell premium like us lions that eat you and feed on your reckless habits. Because you are weak. Because you choose, consciously and unconsciously, not to get stronger. Because you spend all of your days in stock message boards where people know nothing. Because you fear people like myself who will so easily throw this in your face and you will call me the problem because you have no accountability to yourself."

"Accountability... huh, Noel?" I murmur. He just took me down with his words and I don't like it.

I feel beaten down.

So I get down on my knees. I get down on my fucking knees and I look up at him. Now he's really looking down at me.

Looking down at me like the piece of shit that he makes me feel that I am.

And then I do it.

I can't help myself.

I know it's dirty, and wrong, and ... well, everything else, but I do it anyway. I unzip his pants. Slowly. The zipper makes the loudest noise in the silence. I hear him catch his breath. I rub my hand over his crotch, up and down, at first fast, but then slow. Teasing him, and he's as hard as a rock.

"Who's going to be accountable for this, Noel?" I ask, looking up at him with big wondering eyes, my voice low, seductive.

"Jolette, stop."

"Stop?"

I look up at him again while I pull out his one-eyed snake. It's looking right at me eagerly, and I wrap my lips around it.

I suck. Gently. Just to get him even rock harder. "I'll stop, Noel," I say, stopping. He runs his fingers through my long hair and brings my face to his cock again.

I put my lips around him and suck again, going up and down the shaft, taking him in deeper, and he leans his head back against the wall, powerless.

And I've got him.

I've got him, right here, right now.

I keep going, deeper and deeper, pulling his pants down so they're around his ankles, and I reach my hands around to his back, pulling him toward me, sucking harder, moving my fingers in between that little area between his cock and his ass and I make a fist and press, and he gasps involuntarily. He's enjoying this and I wait to see the perfect amount of pressure that he likes.

It's like trading, really, when you buy and watch a stock tick up, but it gets hammered down with a big red candle because somebody on the other side is short, and I press harder but instead of pulling away, I feel his legs spread wider...and he likes it...and his voice, his moans ... go higher. Like the way a stock goes higher... when you're on the right side of a trade.

"Jolette, Jolette," now he's calling my name, and I suck more and more, and then I stop and look up at him.

I watch the agony in his eyes as he pleads, "No, keep going, just a little longer..."

"I thought you wanted me to stop," I whisper innocently. As if I don't know what I'm doing but that statement is so very wrong because I know exactly what I'm doing.

"I was wrong," he says.

"You were wrong?" I ask louder than I should have, because that's all I want to hear. Is that he's *wrong*.

He nods.

"You are wrong, Noel," I repeat. "Very wrong."

"I know, oh God, I know."

He throws his head back against the wall in ecstasy as I take him in my mouth again, showing him no mercy, cupping his balls, squeezing them tighter and then I hear it, "Oh, ohhhhhhhhhh, yes, babyyyyyyyy."

And in this position, in this dark and dirty bathroom, on my knees, with his cock lunged all the way in the back of my throat, where I feel him, pulsating, and thrashing… I feel… the most powerful of all.

It's over, and he pulls me up.

This was always a time bomb ready to explode and now it has, and now what?

I stand there and face him. He pulls out his handkerchief and wipes my face. He stares into my eyes with … admiration, and lust, and …. as I look back at him, there's an innocence I see. One I've never seen or felt with him before.

And he just stares at me.

I stare back at him.

"We're not short Sequenom," he says. "Rick just said that to throw off some of the guys."

"Why?"

"They've been trading the names in their personal account and that's not allowed. He's teaching them a lesson. You're not trading these in your PA, are you?"

"No, of course not."

"Okay, don't."

He starts kissing my neck, and I nod, as I take this all in. And now I want *him all in*.

He brings his lips to mine and kisses me. I feel his tongue playing with mine, going slow, and it's making me so wet, and this is getting a little too intimate, and a part of me wishes he would just spin me around and bend me over and fuck me from behind over the toilet, like a Viking, like somebody who just drills it into me, and all I feel is sweet, exquisite pain mixed with… powerlessness because then I will feel something, instead of this hallow shell of which I have become.

He's pushing his hips against mine and now he's hard again, and he lifts my skirt up and he's kissing my neck with such passion, with an eagerness that I never even knew existed in him, and he whispers in my ear, "I want you...Jolette..."

And because we are almost the same height, I reach down for him and bring him to me, and he takes a condom out of his wallet, slips it on, and slips it in, and I gasp...

Oh, God the feeling of him inside of me... I squeeze, and buck my hips against his, finding his rhythm, and matching it, and then he just stops, and stares at me, and we just stand still like that.

I look into his eyes and it's the most incredible moment. It says way too much, it's far too intimate, and he breathes, and suddenly I remember that scene in Chinatown with Angela, and the way they breathed together.

I'm jealous now but it's also turning me on, and I ask him, "Is this what it's like with Angela? Is this how you fuck her?"

He grabs my hair and pulls it back, hard, and he's hurting me. "Don't talk to me like that."

He starts thrusting, as if shutting me up with his body, moving faster, and I want to control the pace but I can't because he is moving so fast now inside me and then I tilt my hips and he's so hard now, and he hits it in that spot and ... I ... I start coming... and ... oh, god, oh, God, "Noel, Noel!!!!!!"

And it lasts and lasts and lasts...

He looks back into my eyes one final time as we go over the brink together... He has his power back, or so it seems, and he pulls out, zips up his pants, and walks out.

I stand there, breathless. For a second, I can't even believe the whole thing happened.

I pull my skirt down and I walk over to the sinks, turn on the water, and splash cold water on my face.

I look at myself in the mirror and I look like a contented, crazy, but wild, satiated animal. It's that feeling of having rich crème cakes, delicious when you're having them, but you feel sick afterwards because they're not good for you and not sustaining, and you're hungry moments later, craving more.

I feel I'm already hooked. Already hooked on Noel, now on a whole new level, one that could potentially bring me down, and as I leave the ladies room, Paul Zucker is waiting outside.

I'm shocked to see him and the floor that we're on is completely empty which means he was probably there the whole time, and listening the whole time, and all he says is, "He's going to hurt you, Jolette."

I brush past him, and keep moving.

36

Chapter 36

When I get home, my cat is standing in the doorway with a look on his face that says: *It's a good thing you're home. Something is wrong.*

I'm not sure what it is. I move through my apartment and I hear water dripping… I look down at the floor, and there's water everywhere.

I look up, and it's coming from the ceiling.

I rush upstairs and my neighbor's door is wide open. Hundreds, if not thousands, of marijuana plants are everywhere. His apartment is covered in them. "What happened?" I ask. "What the hell is going on?!"

"Hey, Jolette, yeah man, so sorry … My freaking irrigation system imploded."

"What?! Are you growing a marijuana farm in your apartment?" I ask, stating the obvious.

"Uhh, yeah, *was.* But can you not say anything to the landlord? I'll get everything cleaned up and pay for the damage…"

Suddenly, our Chinese landlady comes bursting through the door like the cascading water. "I knew you were badddd! I knew it! I'm evicting you! You doing illegal! Illegal!"

I knew there was something weird going on with this guy for months because I'd always hear him running water at all hours of the night, and I had a sixth sense something was up. I even mentioned it to the landlord in passing, but she shut me down saying, "The walls are thin in these old buildings, and I was "Imagining sounds."

Now here's the proof.

I guess it all comes out in the wash in the end, doesn't it?

I go back downstairs to check on Sam. Cats don't like water and now my apartment is flooded.

The landlord follows me and says that they're going to leave an industrial size fan in my unit overnight to dry things out and they'll replace the carpet in the morning.

"Tomorrow morning?" I ask.

"Yes, we'll have to fix this right away or it'll get mildew."

"But I have to work."

Tomorrow is Friday, and Friday's are the craziest day on the trading desk with options expiration. And Monique is not going to be happy about me missing another day of work.

While my landlady is talking, I snap some photos of the damage and text them to Monique. "Major emergency," I write, "I'll be in late tomorrow." The whole thing seems surreal.

"Luckily," the landlady continues, "I have an extra piece of carpet from the studio that we just renovated on the first floor. It'll fit perfectly in here. You'll love the color and it's stain resistant for your cat."

I look over at poor Sam and he seems nonplussed at everything, he's probably just happy that I'm home, although now he's eyeing the Chinese woman like he wants to lunge for her.

"Okay, okay... Any way we can do this on Saturday, you know, I work during the week and..."

"Saturday!? No. We'd have to pay the workers extra and this will get moldy causing bigger problems. You do not want to wait."

I nod.

"They'll be here tomorrow morning at 8 a.m. and Jolette," she says, as she makes her way for the door, "They are ... how should I put this, really fussy with their work. Do not hover over them, okay? They do not like that at all."

I just stare at her trying to comprehend everything.

"Okay."

* * *

Brittany calls and saves the day and tells me to sleep at her place. I haven't seen her for months, and I take her up on her offer.

I didn't want to leave my cat alone another night, but I didn't want to bring him with me either because he was already traumatized from being with Troy.

Kissing his little lips goodbye after taking a hot shower and putting clean clothes in an overnight bag, I make my way over to Brittany's. She only lives a few blocks away, and I'm excited to see my best friend.

37

Chapter 37

When I get to Brittany's apartment, I knock on her door, and when she opens it, I'm surprised to see her dressed to the nines. She's wearing a knock-out dress, high heeled boots, and her face is filled with makeup. She looks beautiful. *Stunning.*

"Wow," I say, "If you're trying to impress me, you've succeeded. I know it's been a while since we've seen each other, but you didn't have to go through so much trouble," I tell her jokingly.

"Jolette, I tried calling your landline before you left but I must have missed you. I was invited to Mario Lambino's party at the new opening of Posh!"

"What? Posh?" I have no idea what she's talking about.

"Yes! That new clothing store on Union Street! It's opening next week and every top photographer is going to be there tonight for their pre-launch party. They just invited the top modeling houses to go and it's the 'see and be seen' event to be at."

"Really?" This is the last thing on earth I feel like doing.

"Oh Brittany, I thought we were going to put our pajamas on, sit on the couch, eat ice cream, and catch up."

"No! Not tonight. This is too big to miss... Come over to my closet,

I already have some outfits picked out for you."

I hesitantly walk over to Brittany's massive clothes closet.

"I was thinking of this red dress or this pink glittery one..." she says, holding up both dresses and grinning.

"Brittany, those are kind of loud, and seriously? I don't want to go to this."

"I know you don't, Jolette, but you'll do it for me. If Mario sees me and likes me, I could land on the cover of Vogue. It's happened to some of the other girls. Now let's get cracking. Find a dress you like and put it on! We're going!"

Fine. I'll be a dedicated team player for my friend.

Twenty minutes later, I'm standing in front of Brittany's mirror wearing her navy blue velvet dress. It's very tight on me and it's too long because Brittany is a giant but she solves this problem with a large belt that she slaps around my waist. Then she pulls the dress up so it's over my knees.

The boots that she gives me are three sizes too big but because they're boots, they're not slipping off my feet too badly.

"You look good," she says, hurrying me along.

"How long do we have to stay?"

She curls my hair so it's long and streaming down my back. "Just a few hours. It's going to be great, let's go!"

* * *

Brittany tells me that she'll pay for the cab on the way over, and she's already had two vodka/sodas while I was getting dressed and she's manic, talking about her new modeling jobs and all the money that's rolling in.

"That's great, Britt, I'm so happy for you. You really deserve it," I keep telling her over and over again, but I'm wondering if she evens hears me.

We arrive to Posh, and it's a media circus. There are some B list stars, a red carpet, and a line around the block to get in. Brittany leads us to the velvet rope, her name is on the list, and we're let right inside.

It's a scene of all scenes and jammed packed with beautiful people. Model after model stand and hold champagne. The DJ is spinning music and people are posing taking selfies.

Brittany embraces another model she knows, quickly introduces me, and then gets caught up in a group of photographers wanting to take her picture with the other girls.

I'm cast off to the side and I feel left out. I was hoping to tell Brittany what happened between Noel and I and get her opinion. She's my best friend and knows me better than anyone, but I guess now, it will just have to wait.

As I gaze around the room, I realize this industry has its own pecking order like the financial services industry... The largest paid photographers vs. the largest paid hedge fund guys, the largest paid models vs. the largest paid brokers... It's its own system, its own machine, and one I know very little about. I take it all in, watching, feeling like an outsider again.

And then across the room... I see it.

Noel Sheffield... He's talking with three models. He stands with Paul Zucker and four other Wall Street guys.

I stand back and watch him.

He's in his glory, laughing, with his hand on one of the blonde model's back. I observe the way he smiles, leans in and listens, making them feel so important with a never-ending supply of charming things to say.

I should have figured he'd be here, and not just a few hours before this, his dick was inside of me.

He's out for himself like everybody else.

And this realization devastates me.

I feel hurt and abandoned on every level. I should have never allowed myself to fall for him. Like Monique said, and even *Brittany said,* "He's a user, a *narcissist...*"

As I continue to watch him, I wonder who he'll be sticking it to tonight. Maybe he'll take the whole group down to Chinatown and bring Angela into the party.

Who knows?

Who cares.

I start to walk out, trying to find Brittany... and suddenly Robbie Firestone from ABLX stops me, "Hey Jolette, what's up!?"

He's high as a kite, and I don't want to stand and talk to him. I just want to go home. And then suddenly, Noel taps my shoulder and I turn around and look into his eyes.

He's smiling. "Hi, what are you doing here?"

I'm not smiling. I'm like a deer in the headlights with both Robbie and Noel waiting on an answer from me.

"I'm... with my friend."

Brittany stands with some other Wall Street brokers and she waves me over. I watch Noel and Brittany smile at each other.

"Umm, something came up, I have to go."

As I make my way through the crowd, Noel follows me. Outside on the street, I don't have any money for a cab, and I look like a cheap whore in this dress.

"Jolette, Jolette, wait!"

He turns me around and I face him. I'm embarrassed. I don't want to look him in the eyes. My behavior earlier on my knees in that dirty bathroom is inexcusable and I realize Paul is right, I do use sex like a tool. And it's *wrong.* I'm not even sure what came over me.

"I had a good time before," Noel says, still smiling. "That was pretty wild." His eyes are lit up and he's one hundred percent focused on me even though models are pouring out of SUV's and walking past us. "Where are you going?"

"Home."

"What's wrong?" he asks.

"Nothing."

We're standing there, it's weird and I don't know what to say.

"Tell me…"

"It's just… I thought I was going to be hanging out with my friend tonight but she was more interested in going to this party…"

"It's a great party," he says, gazing around and then he looks down at his watch. "I have to get going. I'm on a red eye flight tonight to New York and I'm leaving for the airport now. Do you want me to drop you off?"

He's leaving for New York now...? He just returned from Dubai.

Well, maybe the break will be good for us.

There is no "us." I remind myself.

I nod. "Sure, thanks."

Noel moves to the valet, finds his ticket, and as we wait for his car, model after model pass him saying "Hey, Noel," "Hi Noel!" over and over again.

He knows everybody.

I stand back and watch the parade.

He drives me home, not talking, and then he stops in front of my apartment. "Take care of yourself, okay? Play it cool, and just keep bringing in more accounts. You can keep going to Society meetings if you want, but I can keep you abreast of any movements if you'd rather not go when I'm not there, okay?"

I look at him. I'm so nervous. His eyes *just penetrate me* in the craziest way and as I get out of the car, he reaches for my hand. "We'll go out to dinner when I get back, okay? I'll look forward to it."

I nod. "Okay, Noel, thank you," is all I say.

I get out, and he rushes around the car to open my door for me, which I did not expect.

Sometimes I feel so small around him, and other times, I feel that I can rule the world.

When will I find the happy medium?

He stands there gallantly as I step out.

I want him to kiss me.

I don't think he will.

I have no idea where I stand with him.

A part of me thinks he's just using me as a pawn in his scheme.

But I'm falling in love with him.

Hopelessly, pathetically falling in love with Noel Sheffield.

He leans in and kisses my check, and then he turns to leave.

"Do you have to go, Noel?" I ask.

He turns back to me, and nods.

I walk toward him again, "Are you sure?" I look up, into his eyes. I don't want him to leave.

"Yes, tough girl. It's a quick trip, what's gotten into you?"

He eyes me, wondering.

I try to brush it off. "Okay, have a safe trip, then, bye."

38

Chapter 38

I slept in the kitchen on the floor that night; it was the only part of my apartment that wasn't wet, and I woke up with a sore neck and back.

I started moving my stuff out into the hallway at 6:30 a.m. so when the workers arrived at 8:00 a.m., they could quickly go to work.

The whole thing is an inconvenience but there's no use crying over it now. It happened, the carpet's ruined, and the only thing to do now is to move forward.

The loud commercial size fans running all night made it nearly impossible to sleep but I'll get my apartment fixed and life will go on. At least nobody was hurt.

The two workers are pleased with the job I did, and when they arrive, they move the big things that I couldn't move, like the bed and the couch, out into the hallway.

I sit out on a chair with my cat in my lap, as they go to work. I'm surprised when I notice their age. Both of them are in their seventies, and I wonder how they can endure this manual labor as I observe them haul their heavy supplies, equipment, carpet, carpet padding, and even a commercial size vacuum cleaner into my apartment.

I stay out of their way, and watch the market from my phone as I wait. It keeps me occupied, and the hours pass by quickly.

Bed, Bath and Beyond has gapped up 30% premarket on a new e-commerce deal, and I sold the last of my position a few days ago. If only I held on a little bit longer, I would have gotten close to breakeven.

But isn't that the way it always works, though? The second you sell something you've held ad nauseam at a severe loss, it pops. As if the Wall Street Gods know – *you were weak. You sold at the low. You sold when we bought. And look at us now... winning AGAIN.*

I started to hate the market with every fiber of my being.

Even SOS, that Chinese blockchain company that I held at 15, took a slow, painful demise to a dollar, after announcing another capital raise.

It all makes me sick.

I look up as the workers pass me. They're already working up a sweat, carrying out the old wet carpet, and hammering down the new one, and I see my computer sitting in the hallway lying in wait with the big POISON sign on it and the words: NO TRADING.

It's easy not to trade when you don't have any money left.

Rick still hasn't paid me, and the salary I'm making at ABLX Securities barely covers the rent and groceries. It's no way to live.

I'm holding Sequenom and it's rising but not fast enough to get me out of this hole. I still owe my father money.

I longed to quit the job. I longed to tell Monique goodbye even though things were getting better between us.

I'll wait until I get that $800,000 Rick owes me, and then I'll stop day trading, I promise myself.

I'll pay my father back and I'll invest in annuities or something conservative. Something with staying power. Something that won't implode.

Yes, this is a great plan.

It's all going to work out, I tell myself, and by the time I realize that

I just solved 99% of my problems by deciding not to trade anymore, the carpet is done.

I get off my chair and when I walk inside to see it, it's beautiful! They already moved my bed and the couch back into my studio, and I couldn't believe it! The results were outstanding! "Wow!" I stammer, "It looks great! Thank you!"

I put Sam down in the bathroom, and then I take off my shoes and run into the kitchen to get them some cold juice drinks that luckily, I had on hand. "Here you go, nice cold drinks for you! Thank you! This is amazing!"

I am so relieved. The new carpet is a magnificent shade of silvery blue. That ugly brown carpet that I lived with for years was deplorable, and now it's gone. My mind has been so buried in trading, and trying to make a living, that I never stopped long enough to think, "Hey, maybe it's time for an upgrade."

The mess that the neighbor made upstairs ended up being a blessing in disguise. The workers are playing music that they brought with them, and they're even wearing booties on their feet to protect the new carpet, and I'm elated.

I walk over to their radio and I turn up the volume. A song from the 70's is playing, and I start dancing. I start dancing right there in the center of my apartment, and say, "Come on, dance with me!"

They look at me like I'm crazy but I'm spinning around, waving my arms in the air, swaying my hips and I grab one of their hands and they twirl me around. Then they really start to get into it, and the three of us just start dancing our brains out.

These are the real heroes, I realize, as I dance.

These are *the real men* who get their hands dirty and fix things, and make the world a better place.

I realize I needed a whole new overhaul of my life and my perspective. I need desperately to get away from Wall Street.

It has me in its grip, the grip of greed and always wanting more, and of never being satisfied.

We keep dancing, and for the first time in a long time, maybe in my whole life, I feel free.

39

Chapter 39

"What kind of fill is that?!" I'm pacing back and forth on the trading desk, waiting for a response.

"Jolette, you asked me to pick up 250,000 shares of Cisco at the market, right? Look at time and sales."

"Fuck time and sales! I gave you this order three and a half minutes ago! The clients are not putting up with this! What's taking so long?!"

Silence. A long pause."It wasn't four..."

"Yes, it was! I'm going to lose this account!" And for a second, I realize I sound just like Monique.

"I don't know what you want me to do, Jo- ."

"Change the fucking print! That's what I want you to do. Otherwise, I'll come down there and I'll have him change it myself."

"Okay, Jolette. Geez," he sighs.

The trader calls back and they changed the print and I should have felt better, but I didn't. I am the middle man between the market makers and the clients and everybody is trying to screw everybody. It's getting old.

Kimberly and Robbie eye me as I take off my headset and it slams down on the desk.

"It'll be okay, Jolette," Monique asserts.

I turn to her, not realizing she was watching me. "Yeah."

A certain compatibility has developed between us over the past few weeks. Orders continued to pour in, and with my newfound pipeline of information, we were hitting all kinds of records.

Different as we were in background and age, Monique and I have become at ease with one another, almost intuitively sensing the other's anguish.

Acting as a sales trader to her accounts, her business was booming. I have fully asserted myself into work and with business reaching unprecedented levels, each day has grown longer than the previous one. I'm handling all of the client paperwork, the wiring of their funds, and in the evenings, I attend client events on Monique's behalf.

To avoid getting behind in the arduous amount of paperwork, I spent my evenings building up a new system. I began to attack the paperwork with great ferocity and devised an entire new tracking system for Robbie and Kimberly to follow.

Everything was now logged into an Excel spreadsheet, and equally disseminated amongst the team.

The paperwork is handled with speed and efficiency now, and as cumbersome as it was, I sensed that all of this would add up to a great year end bonus. And once Rick's money comes through, this is done.

I close out my day, depositing the remaining files into the cabinet. I kneel down and alphabetize them all one by one. My eyes are burning from staring at the screens all day long.

Lifting my head wearily, I glance up at the clock: 7:00 p.m.

I rise to turn off her computer, and then I take off for another client dinner. Noel is due in from New York tonight.

I'm hoping I get to see him.

* * *

That weekend, Noel surprised me. We didn't get to see each other for the first week that he was back in town; he was too busy with client meetings, but on Saturday, he took me to Napa Valley!

When he arrives at my door Saturday morning, I sweep my arms around his neck and kiss his cheek. I'm so amorous and he circles my wrists with his hands, lowering my arms to my sides."How are you?" he asks, regarding me with utter seriousness.

But I feel myself almost lift off the ground, I'm so happy to see him.

We drive up to Napa and enjoy the beautiful tranquil scenery. The tight linear valley is framed by tree-covered mountains and a delightful landscape of wildflowers and grapevines that spread across miles of rolling hills and vineyards.

Days like today make me feel grateful to be alive. This is why we worked hard, why we made money, to spend it with somebody... dare I say it, we love.

I know I really can't say I love Noel yet but I felt closer to him than anybody. Maybe it's because he's the only guy I know who loves the markets and trading as much as I do.

He holds my hand as we drive through the long, windy roads, and we enjoy the greenery and vineyards that stretch out in Napa Valley for miles and miles and miles.

Passing a fruit stand on the side of the road, we stop and buy cherries, blueberries, and grapes. We rinse everything off with cold water and eat them as we continue on.

"You gonna stay with me?" Noel asks out of no-where.

I smile, still looking out the window, "Of course."

"Even when I'm old and a 'has been?'"

"You'll never be a 'has been,' Noel."

"I may be someday," he replies. "I'll lose my energy, my drive, my clients..."

"The clients?" I repeat. "Ha! That will be a good thing."

"Yes," Noel agrees distantly, "maybe you're right."

After stopping at Francisco Ford Coppola's winery and enjoying some wine tasting, we continue North on U.S. Route 101.

Noel turns onto West Dry Creek Road in Northern Sonoma and it's one of the most incredible wine drives in the United States.

When the sun sets, he pulls into the Farmhouse Inn, an intimate bed and breakfast. We pass multi-tiered fountains and clusters of tables and chairs hidden beneath protective umbrellas. It has yellow clapboard siding and a front veranda that makes it look simple at first glance, but inside its wonderfully sophisticated, merging rural with contemporary.

We're offered homemade soaps and warm oatmeal cookies when we check in.

I feel my cell phone ringing and I want to make sure it's not my brother, and see that Monique is calling. I have no idea why she's contacting me on a Saturday but I step away and answer. "Hello?"

"Jolette, we can't locate five hundred million in one of the cash accounts for Benson."

"Five hundred million? Did you check with Robbie? He could have sent another wire."

"Okay, I'll check."

"If he didn't, check that Excel spreadsheet I created. Everything should be logged there."

"Okay, okay, I will thanks," she replies, and clicks off.

I return to the front desk and Noel is holding a key and he wraps his arm around me.

"I'm giving you our deluxe Barn Room," the manager says, "It's located in the wooded area at the rear of the property. It's very quiet and private."

"Thank you," Noel replies, and hands over his black Amex. There is no discussion of price.

CHAPTER 39

We walk down the winding path towards the back and find the room and go in. For a moment, I think of that brief conversation with Monique. *That much money is missing from a Benson account? What the hell?*

But as I look around the room, the wine-red curtains, dark-wood accents and ornate chandelier make it easy to imagine that I'm in the vineyards of Spain and far away from the world of Monique. The room has an outdoor deck and a stone fireplace, and there's a lavish marble bath and a whirlpool tub that's positioned by the windows and it overlooks the deck.

The king size feather bed has a white scalloped canopy and a thick white comforter that looks like a cloud.

Noel takes out his cell phone and does something I've never seen him do before, he turns it off.

We take off our clothes, pull back the blankets, and jump into bed. Reaching for each other, we begin kissing like new lovers. Noel rolls on top of me and explores my face with his hands. "You're beautiful."

I'm barely breathing, staring at his lips, studying their shape, and he takes in my face, his fingers strong against my skin, and kisses me again, firmer this time, more certain.

He takes me right then and there and makes love to me slowly, painstakingly slow, and hours later, he buries his face in the perfumed cloud of my hair which is spread out all over the pillows.

It's the scene from the greatest romance novel that you've ever read in your whole entire life.

And I've never been happier.

* * *

The next morning, Noel brushes the hair away from my face and kisses my ear. "Good morning," he says with a grin, as sunshine bursts through the window.

I don't have to look at him to know that his eyes are filled with lust.

He pulls me toward him and his hair is messed, his five o'clock shadow is growing in, and he looks dangerous, like a bad boy; the kind of guy you never get over.

I take this photo of him with my mind, hoping that it's not an image that will haunt me for all the rest of my years.

For I've finally given in to the irresistible charts, I mean, *charms,* of Noel Sheffield.

40

Chapter 40

That morning, Noel and I have breakfast outside on the veranda, and I'm wearing a white, pretty sundress. We're served fresh eggs, bacon, roasted potatoes and warm bread that arrives straight out of the oven. The strawberry jam is homemade, and Noel puts it on a fresh warm almond croissant, and hands it to me.

I take a bite, swallow it down with the blackest of coffee, and I'm in heaven. It's better than a dream.

Noel Sheffield is perfect. He is calm and strong and doesn't talk too much to overwhelm me. Oftentimes, we just sit together and enjoy the silence. And to sleep in after waking up at 3 a.m. everyday is a gift like no other. You never appreciate that until it's taken away from you. I never got used to working Wall Street hours on the West coast. My body never adjusted.

But now my body is rested, and satiated.

I have everything I want.

And it simply doesn't get better than this.

* * *

Noel leaves for the restroom, and the waitress walks by, leaving a copy of Barron's on the table. "The man who was sitting here requested this. Would you mind giving it to him?"

"Sure, thank you."

I stare at Barron's lying on the table and it's *the reminder of our lives; the ups and downs of the market, and it's all resuming again tomorrow.*

I turn the paper around so I can read the headlines. Barron's is known for its breaking stories and it only comes out on Sunday's. I know Noel is an avid reader because he has copies at his house and he's always quoting the articles in one form or another.

When I see the front page, I cannot believe it — A large photo of CEO Bryce Mallone of AdventureWorld stares back at me. And when I see the headlines, I almost throw up my entire breakfast.

"CEO Bryce Mallone Dies In A Private Plane Crash. Accident? Or Malice?"

I read the article: "Beloved AdventureWorld CEO dead at 51... Suspicious activity is being investigated..."

I pull out my cell phone and check the stock message boards: "The CEO's plane: How did it go down? Who's Behind It?" "Congrats to the shorts!" Another message: "Easiest short play in the world: take down the CEO's plane."

I pull up another article. A blog: "They Killed the CEO. They Did it For Money."

I struggle to make sense of it all, staring at the articles, their amount and complexity overwhelming.

Noel sits back down at the table, and I look up at him. *Does he know about this?*

Does the Society have something to do with this?

Bryce did not come through with his portion of the Sequenom deal.

Was this his punishment?

Death?

Did they kill him?

Noel reaches for the newspaper, his face a cold mask. "I need to see that for a second."

Of course he does.

I watch his face as he reads the article. Not surprised. No remorse. Nothing.

He looks back at me.

I sit in stunned silence.

He doesn't say anything.

"Did you know about this?" I ask.

"I..." he stammers.

"Did you know, Noel?" I repeat. This time my voice is firm.

His face goes red.

My jaw drops.

I look around. And suddenly, my life which was a dream, just turned into an epic nightmare.

There's a couple sitting right next to us peacefully eating breakfast, and Noel turns to me. "Let's talk about this in the car, okay? Are you ready to go?"

I get up. I'm dizzy.

For a second, I can't move.

We make our way back out to the car in silence. The Lamborghini is bright and shiny in the parking lot. Noel opens the door for me.

I can't look at him. I get in the car in biggest confusion and shock of my life.

* * *

Noel is not talking but he keeps getting texts, and he keeps responding, and this is upsetting me because, (a) I'm sure it's about the CEO and

(b) He's not telling me anything. And (c) We've almost crashed three times.

Yet I'm starting to think the less I know, the better. "Can you call Rick for me, right now Noel, and ask him what's taking so long with my money?"

I'm starting to feel suffocated with my life, as if it's weaved in so tightly with Noel and this Society that I'm beginning to feel convinced that I can't handle it anymore. "Do it now."

Noel is not a guy who takes orders but he hits Rick's number on speed dial and puts the call on speakerphone.

"Yeah, Noel," Rick answers.

"I have Jolette here in the car with me," Noel begins, which I'm sure is a.k.a. for: Don't announce any secrets right now, "and she wants to know when she's getting her money."

"Let me check, hang on."

Rick puts him on hold and Noel turns to me with a look that says: See how hard I work for you?

"The funds will be available in her account in the next twenty-four hours," Rick assures him, and then he clicks off.

Noel pulls off the 101. "See. There you go," he mollifies with a tone that amplifies savior.

He turns to me and smiles. "What are you going to do with all that money, huh? Run away?"

There's a hint of seriousness to his voice.

I'd love to run away, I think.

Love to.

He's changed. It's like I'm not even with the same guy I left San Francisco with.

Noel pulls over on some side street and cuts the engine. We're somewhere in between the wine country and San Francisco and I see a little church up ahead.

It looks so peaceful. And as I sit in this car with Noel, I feel anything but peaceful.

Was this his alibi, going away with me this weekend? Get the heat off of him, by getting out of town? I have so many questions and I wonder if I'll ever get any answers.

"Why are we stopped here?"

"I want to talk."

He wants to talk.

I wait for him to say something, *anything*. But then the words just fall from my lips. "I think I'm done with this, Noel."

"Done with what?" he asks. "Us?"

I wasn't expecting that. "No, the Triad. I just … you know, I've been thinking … I just want out. It's been a good run. I'm going to stop trading."

"Out?" he stammers, "Are you crazy, Jolette? There's no *out.*"

"What do you mean?"

"What I mean is — you're one of us now."

There's an anger to his voice and I don't like it. I feel afraid of him now. "One of us?" I mimic. "No, Noel, I'll never be one of "us."

He's not happy with my response and he's losing me.

And then I just blurt it out. "They killed him, didn't they?"

Noel doesn't respond.

"Huh, Noel, what, were they short too? They needed to make five points on a short call, so hey, let's blow the CEO's plane out of the sky and kill him? Is that what happened?" I shake my head. "You know what? I don't even want to know."

Noel doesn't say anything but his silence says it all.

"I want to go into that church over there," I say, and I get out of the car.

It's 2:00 in the afternoon and regular Sunday masses for the day have ended but the church doors are open.

I go inside and take a seat up front. I get on my knees and pray, and find Noel beside me. I feel emotional. I can't believe it's come down to this, and worse, that I'm sitting here with a man I love, and I don't even really know who he is.

After a few moments, I sit back in the pew and listen to the silence. I try my hardest to listen for guidance.

Noel puts his hand on my knee and looks at me. I don't look back at him. I can't. I get up and start to walk out, and as we pass the confessional booth, he takes my arm, and pulls me inside.

He closes the door and we're in a tight little space. It's dark, there's a small window that's open and Noel pushes me against the wall. He turns me around and starts kissing me from behind, whispering in my ear... "I'm sorry..."

And I whisper back, "Why Noel, why?"

I feel his breath in my ear and on my neck, and he starts kissing me more, "I didn't want to bring you this far into this...Forgive me, Jolette. We're going to get through this... okay? Just stick it out..."

"No, Noel, I want out. We can't be in here, let's go."

He lifts up my dress and starts fingering me from behind. I can't believe he's doing this here. He rubs up against me and he's hard and I hear him unzipper his pants. He cups my breasts, and brings my panties down, "Spread 'em, Jolette, do it for me."

"No, Noel, not here..."

"Do it, please baby..."

He reaches into my bra, and I can feel my nipples push and strain against his soft fingers as though they're trying to siphon nourishment from him.

"Noel..."

"Bend over." He takes control with his usual panache, and the sensation of feeling him behind me is like a hot wire against my nerve ends. *Dare I expose myself to him again?*

He reaches for my panties, pulls them down to my ankles. I spread my legs, he thrusts himself inside, and I arch off the ground, crying out his name. Gripping the wall, I mold myself to him as he slides his fingers through my hair, needing something to hold onto, and with every withdrawal, I arch my hips involuntarily to meet his, grinding my body against his, wanting more of him, *needing more of him...*

I clench my thighs together, and I feel the tremors start to shake from within... Noel plunges so deep inside my body, he buries his face in my hair to muffle his shout,"Jo...lette ... Jo... lette... oh God...."

41

Chapter 41

When I get home, the money's already there. The $800,000. Rick's money.

It hit.

It's Sunday night, and I can't trade anything other than crypto, so I start. I sit down at my desk, log into my crypto account, put my lucky red bandana around my head, and I go to work.

I pull up every coin and watch the numbers flashing. Volume is always high; catch a good wave and it's better than sex. *Better than sex, it's better than anything...*

I pick up my mouse and stare at my screen as coins in every name, in every size, flash across my screen. I'm a big fan of Ethereum Classic; it trades mostly like a stock and the chart looks fantastic. It's bucking against the upper trendline after consolidating for about ten days and ready to take off. My timing couldn't be better.

My excitement mounts, my mind works like a machine... and I start to put my orders in.

I go in small at first, picking up 5,000 shares at 55. I remember how this was trading at 8 only a few months ago. It's been on a tear, hitting a high of almost 100.

Come on – give it to me. Fill me...Right here...

My heart races. Adrenalin runs through my body. I've traded and lost before and swore I'd never go back. But when you love somebody or something... *Then it's amazing how willing you are to overlook its problems and its flaws and go back to it again.*

A message pops up: "You bought 5,000 shares ETC, $55."

Yes...

It starts going higher, rising fast, 57... 58.40.... 59.10... I'm in it and buying more and the rush is incredible.

I couldn't remember the last time I sat at my desk and actually traded. *Traded for my own account.*

Had power over my own money.

My own destiny.

I sit in front of my home screens transfixed. Lights flash in green and red. The market is alive... it has a pulse. My hand slides so smoothly over the mouse and I'm so skilled at discovering patterns in the market's daily ebb and flow, I'm rarely wrong. ETC keeps climbing and everything's a blur. I'm moving at warp speed, thinking so fast, working so fast, I can barely breathe. Or maybe I'm breathing for the first time. *Maybe this is what it's like to feel alive.*

ETC keeps running, and I'm a higher than a fucking kite. The rip is so good... it's epic. I'm up 35% in the first hour. I want to let it ride... but I need to clock profit.

It'll go higher, my inner voice says.

It'll *double.*

I stare into my screens, and that dizzying narcotic blur of numbers and charts mesmerizes me, hypnotizes me, and if I play my cards right, I'll *be sitting on a million dollar account within no time...*

No, my other side argues, crypto is volatile, the gains are fleeting. Clock profit, *clock profit.*

But volatility is how the real money is made.

DIAMOND HANDS.

So I keep buying.

ETC.X goes higher. Excitement races through me like fire. My heart pounds with increasing speed. I check the crypto message boards: "Nothing greater than being an ETC bull. Stay the course, people! STAY THE COURSE!! DO NOT SELL!"

I stare back at the chart.

I'm not sure how many hours have passed after this. I'm trading all through the night, and the last time I saw the clock, it read 3:00 a.m.

I remember that it's Monday and I have to go to work, but now I'm up over two million dollars. This thing is on a tear, and I couldn't, wouldn't, tear myself away from it.

I keep watching and I want to run, scream, jump up and down, jump off a building. I needed to do something to keep this adrenaline alive. I don't know how, but I need to do something rash.

I am staring at four million dollars now and I'm so high, so euphoric, I know I can double it to eight.

You're fucking crazy.

And then it all starts to go south.

My throat thickens as reality grips me. I intuitively check the indexes as the whole market starts turning. For a second, I'm held in a vise of the most paralyzing shock. Averaging down, I buy more and more, using up the rest of my money, and then I go on margin.

Everything still drops.

I say a prayer.

And then another.

ETC starts to go up and I start to sell into the momentum... Smaller lots to not crack it in half. But the volume is so huge, I know my tiny trades mean nothing. I'm just a pawn in this, ready to get steamrolled. *Trampled.*

I hear Monique's voice coming through my answering machine:

"Jolette, it's 9:13! Where the fuck are you?!"

The stock market opened and I realize I traded through the morning research meeting. I think I rode out some Bitcoin and then when the real market opened, I decided to go all in on the miners.

Why not.

Why fucking not?

I have plenty of cash now and am still holding the bag on SOS. I have 200,000 SOS at an average of 11.12 and it's trading at 1. It's been stuck here for over three months. I couldn't stand the mother fucking thing. I wanted to trade around it, get out of it, get my money back, show everybody who's boss.

I cash out of Bitcoin and some of my other crypto positions. My account is at $4,030,882. I stare at the numbers. I'm in awe. I'm on fire. I feel bigger than God.

But for some reason, the feeling goes away ... *So fast.*

Why? Where did it go?

Doesn't matter. I buy in SOS. First I plow in with 200,000 shares to get my average down. And I watch as the stock trades sideways... knowing this is probably a big mistake... but unable to stop myself. I hold on to hope... and hope is never a trading strategy... Come on... Come *on...*

SOS starts to tick up. $2.80... $2.96... My average is still over $5.00.

If this follows on the tailwinds of crypto, it will run. Crypto had a blazing run last night – this should be no fucking different.... LET'S GO, PEOPLE! LET'S GO!

I hear my phone still ringing. I ignore it.

My cat comes up onto my desk, nudging against my arm. He's hungry. He needs to eat.

I ignore him too.

I can't peel myself away... I double in again, buying another 200,000 shares... Just for fun. I just want to get down my average ...

That's all I want…

And within the next four hours I'm trading all around this thing. Selling my cheaper positions against the higher ones and clocking cash. Which sort of fucks me because my average remains high. I try to sell on the way up, but my bags are so large – I have pieces as high as $15; it takes forever to put a dent in this colossal disaster of a trade gone awry.

But then I say fuck it. I bet the house, go long 600,000 shares and I don't realize it, but now, I'm on margin. Once the margin money hits, there's no stopping it and I keep buying more and more and keep trading around the position and the stock is moving so quickly, the next thing I know, it hits the high of the day of $7.50 and starts to move down.

Fast.

Like a snow plow falling off a cliff.

I watch.

My money starts to evaporate before my eyes.

First I'm down $300,400… then the loss turns into $440,882, the losses are multiplying so fast, there is no time to even clear out of the way of this falling knife.

I need to wait, need to wait for a bottom, or at least until it stabilizes, but there seems to be no bottom in sight.

I can feel my heart racing. My arms are getting sweaty. My breath is quick, and I feel like I can't catch it.

I'm now down $1,500,333 and I get up. I walk away. Fuck. *That SOS was always a piece of shit.*

Why did I get caught up in trading it again?

Why couldn't I just accept the loss and let it go?

No. I will win.

I sit back down at my desk.

I watch. And wait.

There's something in losing money that feels so familiar to me. *You really are a useless, worthless piece of shit is the message I get from it.*

The stock stabilizes and I try to buy more. But I realize I'm out of margin money. I'm all in and this thing is dropping.

I am not sure what to do. Sell and take the hit, or pray?

I do the latter, as my head tells me, *Noel never loved you. He's going to leave you... Just like everybody else.*

The stock drops more.

You can't hold on to him. The end is inevitable. He doesn't want you. He never wanted you.

He will never love you.

It's all a game he's playing.

I pick up my mouse, my hands shaking. I feel like I'm about to cry... or scream... or run... or faint. Or smash something. I need water or juice, or something in my stomach.

I feel sick.

I'm so alone and isolated.

I want to fucking die.

* * *

I'm on the floor in my bathroom. I got a margin call. I blew all the fucking money. I lost everything. I can't even remember the balance. SOS went from $7 back down to $1.91 in a matter of three hours.

Who the fuck knows what happened this time? Or why.

But I am done.

I have nothing.

I am nothing.

Without my money, without my trading, I can't survive. I can't breathe.

I can't cope with life.

I'm holding a bottom of pills in my hand. I can hear my cat meowing but I am not sure where he is. I am dizzy and think I have thrown up. I can't remember. I stare at the lights at the overhead ceiling and if I concentrate long enough, I can only see white and pretend that I am in heaven. *I'm in heaven with my mother.*

I open the bottle and there are only a few more pills left. I take them but I can't swallow them. My mouth is so dry.

I haul myself up by my knees and lean over the sink and turn on the faucet. I run the water and put my hand underneath it to splash water into my mouth. *Go down.*

Go down!! I swallow.

I fall back onto the floor.

And wait for escape.

* * *

Opening my eyes, I am unaware of the hour, and my head is piercing with pain. It feels like the Empire State building decided to move in on my forehead. I can't move. I realize I am lying in a puddle of my own vomit.

I don't know why, but I see Noel.

His face. His blue eyes staring down at me.

I must be dreaming. I close my eyes because I can't keep them open.

And then I remember… the money.

The money is gone.

* * *

I wake up hours later. I have no idea what happened. I glance at the clock, its 12:25 a.m.

What happened?

42

Chapter 42

I get off the bus in Chinatown and head up Stockton Street, pushing through people. I can't see, everything's blurry... *How did I do it? Why... Why... How .... Holy shit, holy fuck, I'm dead.*

I want to die.

I want to kill myself.

I have to take myself out of this pain.

It's 2:00 in the morning, I can't sleep, my heart is racing, I feel sick.

Sicker than I've ever felt.

I had to blow the money again... Didn't I? How? I try to play over again in my head what happened... the market opened... I missed work... I started trading marijuana stocks... they opened and gapped up... I bought at the high, they came straight down. The chart on the daily was they just got fucking hammered. I sell at the low, take a 30% hit... then I think I was trading the miners ... off a crypto run... and then I plowed into an obscure technology name... I chase that because that was running up too... and then the fall.... It starts to fall, I bought more on margin... more and more but it kept going down and down... And then I plowed back into SOS...

And then the margin call, they sold me out.

That's all I remember... I was up trading crypto. I was up big ... my account was over a million dollars...or was it four? I don't remember.

What fucking happened...?

How could I blow $800,000 in the course of 24 hours...?

Who does that?

Who else gets burned that bad...

Fuck, I'm dead.

Dead.

Everything is blurry. I see the faint colors of the Chinatown signs and the different languages that never made sense to me... I don't know why I'm here... *Chinatown*... and then I remember.

Angela.

I want to see her.

I need to see if it was all lies.

Did he sleep with her?

And was he lying about it? Because the lie hurts more than anything.

It's the lying that's the ultimate betrayal.

I have to know.

Maybe she can help me.

Maybe she can give me an elixir to fix me.

I have to find out.

I want to feel what Noel feels when he's with Angela. Noel always wins. Noel always comes out on top.

I want to. Be. Noel.

* * *

I arrive to the dilapidated building, the one I showed up at with Noel just a few months ago... and how much can change? *How much can a person go down the rabbit hole in a few months?*

You never changed, an inner voice tells me.

You had a gambling problem then, and you still have one now.

The stakes got just bigger, that's all.

And now... you may *never come back.*

The wreckage is too severe... the damage too horrendous.

No, no.

I always come back.

I push my way inside the building and avoid all the Chinese men... I think I'm crying but I don't know... I feel that my face is wet, but maybe something fell on me outside... I don't know and I don't care...

I must find her.

Find Angela.

Somebody, a Chinese man, tries to stop me. I brush past him, unstoppable in this brothel. Chinese people are being entertained with music, dancing and erotic titillation. In another room, workers are being taught the art of lovemaking before graduating as professionals. I'm restless, looking around. And then I see her.

Same spot as before.

That same red dress.

I can never forget her.

She is beautiful, like a China doll. White, pale skin, and bright red lipstick. Jet black straight, long hair.

I go up to her.

"Remember me?" I ask.

She just stares into my eyes. I'm almost hypnotized by hers. *Her eyes.* She doesn't say anything, just stares back at me, and the Chinese man who tried to stop me before intervenes and asks her something in Chinese.

He's angry, worried for her.

She shakes her head: *No.*

I don't know what they're saying to each other.

I don't speak Chinese.

I know nothing about the culture and never cared to but suddenly, I want to know everything. And everything about Angela... *What is her secret?*

"Come," is all she says, leading me through a door.

I follow.

We are in the dark caves again, moving, and they are gray and old and hollow. It still gives me the creeps but I'm not afraid. I can't sink any lower than I've already sunk.

I am at a bottom. *So what's there to be afraid of?*

I hope she gives me enough drugs where I overdose.

I really want to die.

Nobody would find me down here.

Nobody.

I'm starting to wonder if this is my smartest move.

But I can't remember what it's like to make a smart move. Because all of my moves have been bad.

Very bad.

Getting worse by the second.

Angela leads me into a room where there's a massage table. "Get on," she points to the table. I sit on it and look at her. Again into her eyes.

I put my hand on her neck. I just want to touch her, to feel her skin. I play with her hair, wrap it into my fingers. She closes her eyes. She has almost a sexual response to it. I get off the table and stand face to face with her.

I reach in and kiss her lips. Slowly, barely touching them... I'm getting wet, she let's me kiss her, and I feel her tongue on mine, it's so soft and wet and I've never felt another girl's tongue like that. "Let me touch you, Angela," I say, pushing my hands around her back, moving down to her ass, pushing me to her. I unbutton the little black buttons on her red dress…

One by one, they open.

Louder her little murmurs get. Her eyes are closed and I open up her dress. I remove her breasts and they hang out of her bra. They're beautiful. Big and round, and she's such a slim girl. I start to touch, then lick them. She let's me, she likes it.

"You enjoying this?" she asks me.

I nod.

I want more.

I want all of her right now.

I want to disappear in her.

I want to feel what Noel feels when he's with her.

And then she stops me, and asks, "How much are you going to pay?"

I freeze and look back at her. "Pay for what?"

"For this," she whispers in my ear, moving her hands onto my breasts through my shirt. She lifts my shirt up over my head, and then touches her breasts to mine. The feeling is incredible. I don't want her to stop.

But I'm not paying her anything.

A little grin comes across my face. "Pay you?" I ask. Playing with her, running my thumb around her breast and squeezing her nipple. "How about you pay me?"

I'm a little angry now.

How dare she?

She moves over to the corner of the room where's there's a bureau. She reaches into the drawer and pulls some items out. A pipe, some liquid, some powder. She mixes it and I watch, as she lights two candles.

The candles bring a soft lighting to the room. You can hear the echo of everything's that's happening above in Chinatown, all the shenanigans, all the betting, all the deals, all the foreplay.

But down here where we are, it's quiet. We're hidden. And it's just the two of us. She comes over to me with the concoction, puts some into the pipe, lights it and inhales.

"You have some dark energy," she says. "This will help you get clear, open up your chakras."

I take the pipe in between my lips and inhale. It feels great, I feel great. I feel no more pain anymore, none at all. And I feel like I can stay here forever with Angela in this little dark cave and smoke her magic and just make love to her. I wanted to make love to her. I wanted to … I wanted to … I wanted to…

"Does Noel still come to see you?" I ask.

She gives me a confused look. "Noel?"

I nod.

"Oh. Noel. He used to come."

"Not lately?"

She shakes her head, "No."

"Why?"

"He got afraid."

"Afraid of what?"

"Deviant spirituality. Evil value systems promoting the suffering of others."

I take the pipe again, inhale. "…What happened?"

"The foot soldiers betrayed him. He was in a cult tied to illicit narcotics they trafficked across the blockchain…Stakes too high for him. The offerings made to the deities become primeval and barbaric."

I'm so high. So high… I nod. I want to ask her to go on, but I can't speak.

"They tied his friend to a chair, sawed off his legs… and other stuff. Bad."

I can't hear any more of it. I put my hands on her tiny hips and lift her onto the table. "Let's give each other massages."

I needed transcendence from the reality of the human condition. I take one more hit, and feel myself climbing into a warm, fluffy cloud. I smile, "I'll do you first," I say.

She is as light as a feather, she takes five more puffs on the pipe, and lies back. "Make me feel good," she says, lifting off her dress, and she lays there before me in her underwear.

She removes her bra, runs her fingers over her breasts, and takes my hands, moving them onto her.

I massage her. Her breasts feel so warm and soft, and I listen to her breathe, and I move my hands down her stomach. It's flat and soft, and she pushes my hand lower, and I start rubbing that spot between her legs. She spreads them. "Oh, yesss," she says, "that feels so nice."

I watch as she sits up and goes back over to the bureau. She comes back with a brand new vibrator and opens the package, inserts a battery and presses the button. It makes this little noise. She gets back on the table with it and brings it between her legs. She loves it. "This feels like heaven," she says.

She puts my hand on it, and wants me to take over, and she rubs up against it, back and forth. I tilt it, and open her legs wider. "Take it, Angela."

"Oohhhh God..."

Her eyes close, and I watch as she takes as much pleasure out of it as she can, writhing, and coming in a loud, hysterical orgasm.

She pulls me toward her, and I curl up beside her. She stares at the ceiling, and tells me, "If you like that and want to do it again, it will cost you two hundred and fifty dollars."

She gets up and puts her dress back on, and I just stare at her.

"We have to go," she says, "Somebody else is going to need this room."

I look at her.

I think I start laughing, I'm not sure.

And that's how it's done in *Chinatown.*

* * *

She gives me a bunch of pills before I leave, and I'm high as I leave and the lights and the people and the smells outside take on a heightened sense. I don't even know if I can catch a bus this late. I feel dirty and gross, and then I remember… *the money's gone.*

43

Chapter 43

I think I hear someone pounding on the door. Maybe it's Paul wanting to use the phone again. The pounding continues and I can't move, too sick now, too devastated, too broken.

I'm home now and the pounding gets louder, and I wonder if it's my head, and then I realize it's not.

Somebody is definitely trying to get into my apartment.

I don't know who and I don't know why and I don't really care. I'm starting to come to and I don't want to and the pain of remembering the money I just lost is worse than any physical pain I can ever endure.

My eyes are closed, I can't open them if I wanted to, and then I realize, I am in somebody's arms...

I am being cradled like a baby.

I hear Noel's voice.

It must be a dream.

Just another dream.

And then I see him... his blue eyes, they are blurry and then come into focus. "Why?" I hear him ask over and over again.

He lets me go and I stare at him, as if I'm looking at him for the first time. He's leaning over me, he's wearing his glasses and his eyes show concern. Concern, disappointment, but more than anything else, fear. "Why are you doing this to yourself?"

I stare back at him. Glad he is there. But not sure how he got here. He gets up and walks over to my blazing computer screens. "What happened, Jolette? What did you do?"

He turns back to me, and waits for my answer. But I can't answer. I can't. I won't.

"You have to stop," he says, looking at my screens and seeing the devastation for himself. "You really have to stop."

He picks up a bunch of paperwork on my desk. Its bank loans, unpaid bills, debts, all with my name on it. The detritus of my financial problems keeps on coming, the amount and complexity looks like it has him momentary baffled.

"What is this?"

He looks horribly upset.

He comes back over to the floor. Because that's where I guess I am, on the floor, and unfortunately that's where he found me. He holds up the pill bottle. "How many of these did you take?"

I close my eyes. I want more of those pills. Why am I even awake? Does anything work? Or is everything broken, including my pills?

He shakes the bottle in front of me as his voice rises. "How many?!" I try to reach for the bottle. I didn't realize I had more pills, but he pulls his hand away fast. "Do I need to call an ambulance?"

I don't answer.

I'm not sure I can answer.

I can barely see him but I know he's not happy. "That's it," he roars, "I'm calling 911!"

"No! No, Noel, I'm fine."

I try to sit up. I'm so dizzy.

"Look at me, Jolette."

I can't.

"Look. At. Me."

And slowly my eyes focus on him. He looks so handsome there. Still in his suit, always in a suit. Mr. Perfect. Mr. I've got it all under control. Mr. Nothing Can Touch Me. Mr. I'm going to eventually leave you.

"I'm okay," I mutter.

He starts dialing the phone anyway and I smash it out of his hands! "STOP!" I scream. "They'll lock me up! That's my worst fear, to be locked up!"

He watches as the phone scatters across the floor. I lie back down and he comes over and sits down beside me on the floor. He puts my head in his lap. He leans against the wall and cradles me like that, brushing my hair with his hands.

I turn sideways and curl up in a ball, facing him. My face is buried in his stomach; his warm, cushiony stomach, and I feel safe, so safe and comfortable then I remember that it's all gone and it's all going to end and I start to cry.

Sobs.

Big pathetic sobs. "Please Noel, don't go... please..."

He doesn't say anything. He's just staring straight ahead as I look up into his eyes.

"Is that why you did this?"

I don't say anything and I turn away. I'm not sure what he's referring to the pills or the trading... but I don't know how to answer as he repeats the question, "Is it, Jo?"

And when I don't answer he looks down into my eyes. And he says the most truthful thing that he has ever said to me. "This isn't about me. You have a gambling problem. You need to get help."

* * *

The next few hours are spent in a confused haze. Noel doesn't leave my apartment. He bathes me, he feeds me, he puts cold compresses on my head, and lastly, he lays me into bed and puts me under the covers. "I'm going to go," he begins quietly.

And I knew those words were coming, and when I hear them, again I feel like the rug is being pulled out from underneath me.

Why is it so terrifying when he leaves?

I grab his arm like a reflex, and I pull him toward me. I don't say anything, but the desperation in my eyes tells it all. He glares at me, saying "Stop," with his eyes. He moves his arm away, his arm, so big and strong, if it only stayed on me forever, I would be okay. I wouldn't be scared. I wouldn't fear he would leave me and I would never see him again.

"Why..." he begins.

And I know what he's going to say.

I hope he doesn't. But it's coming, I can feel it.

"Why won't... you ...ever let me leave?"

And the tears spring to my eyes as if he just opened a can of warm soda in a hot dessert, and they fall down my face, and I feel like a little baby and I know I'm acting like one, and when he met me, I was so different than this.

I didn't care about people. I never let myself get attached. I was always gone before any real bond could happen.

He waits for my answer which is not typically how he behaves. When I ignore his questions, he just gets up and leaves.

But this time, for whatever reason, he stays. And he waits.

My heart is racing through my t-shirt and it's so loud I'm wondering if he can hear it. I don't know what to say. Or what he wants to hear. Usually I can figure out something and just nail him with it, but now, it's on me, and he's waiting for a God damn answer.

A faint whisper of my own voice says, "You're going to leave... like my mother."

He clears his throat. I think he's pleased with himself that he got an answer but he just stares back at me with hurt, confused eyes. "Your mother?" he pushes. "What happened?"

"...She died."

He waits for me to say more and watches me. But I don't say anything else.

"She did?" he asks finally, probing.

I nod.

"How?"

"Car accident."

The words hang in the air. I don't tell him the whole truth. That I was there in the back seat, talking, and caused her to have the accident. No, I forget all of it, and trading is the only thing that stops it from coming back in my mind.

It is the only. Thing.

That. And Noel.

"How old were you?"

"Six."

"I see. I'm sorry."

He takes me in his arms again and I'm surprised by this. He holds me tight. "I had no idea, that must have been terrible," and when I hear the sadness in his voice, I start to cry even more and I don't want to cry, I want to forget it all, I want to be somebody else, I don't want to be this person tortured by this anymore. I mean how long does a person have to suffer for something that happened in their past?

"And I know if you go, you are going to leave me the same way she did," and now I'm really crying and I've never cried like this, not in front of anybody before at least, and he kisses my head, my ears, my cheeks, my lips...and he whispers in my ear, "I would never leave you like that, I promise..."

And when I see his eyes, I am surprised he is not kissing me and waiting for the passion to ignite and have sex and see that lust in his eyes, no, what I see now, is something totally different.

He is looking at me, and understanding me for the very first time.

And all I see in his eyes is love.

44

Chapter 44

I took four days off from work after my spill, after my fall off the wagon, off the horse, whatever you want to call it, and then I went back into work.

Monique seemed glad to have me back. We landed three more new venture capital accounts and handled ten more distributions. I was able to throw myself back into work, completing the paperwork for Monique faster than anybody else could do it.

I was organized and had answers for Monique the second she asked for them. This was a blessing and a curse because I was her "go to," person again, her right-hand man.

She stopped yelling so much and seemed to have calmed down. The Wall Street firms were cracking down on expenses so the grand trips and dinners became less and less frequent. That didn't bother me whatsoever.

"Jolette!" Monique calls, "I need you to pick up the Pittsburgh endowment on line five!"

I grab the line. "Jolette," the new associate, Connor, sneers, "What happened to the Robinhood IPO? We asked for shares and we didn't get any. When are you guys going to stop screwing us out of deals…

we give you ENOUGH GOD DAMN BUSINESS...."

I let him rant.

And in this moment, I have compassion for him. "I understand, you're frustrated, Connor. I'd be, too."

I can hear a long sigh of relief come on the other end of the line. "That's right, I'm frustrated."

"And they're on you at work, huh?" I say softly, "to bring in more deals...bring up those profits...?"

"Yeah! It's been harder than ever! We had some funds that were short earlier in the year and they got hammered! Thanks to fucking Powell and his rigging of this unbelievable, unstoppable market."

"I get it."

"You're cool, Jolette, you know, I always liked you..."

"Well, just hang in there," I say. At the same time, I pull up the Pot account. This is where the firm keeps hidden IPO shares. You can dip into the POT on an emergency basis only, and I figured this was an emergency. We can't lose accounts now, can we?

"Listen, I just DTC'ed 20,000 shares of the Robinhood IPO to your account. That should help, okay? Stock is slated to start trading around 11 this morning."

"You're the best, Jolette! The bomb! I owe ya! Thanks!"

I hang up, and grab another ringing line.

The IPO opened 55 points higher. Priced at $44, started trading at $99. I'm sure he flipped it right at the open. Over a million dollar profit. For doing nada....

That's just the way it works around here.

I stare at the pile of paperwork that needs to be dealt with, and I know I will probably put in another twenty more hours over the weekend.

But at least I'm not home, day trading.

* * *

I fall asleep the minute my head hits the pillow with my cat by my side, and I am jarred awake by the ringing phone at 1:35 a.m.

"Hello?"

"Jolette, there's an emergency meeting down at the Club," Noel says. "They want us all to meet… right *now*."

"What do you mean?" I ask, sitting up.

"There's an emergency meeting, I'm going to pick you up in ten minutes. Be downstairs."

"No, Noel…I'm… not going."

"You have to. Get dressed, I'm leaving now."

He's leaving now?

Reluctantly, I dress and am downstairs in the pitch dark in ten minutes. His Lamborghini lights flash through the fog, and he pulls over.

I walk out of my building, and get in his car.

Something feels off.

"I don't have a good feeling about this, Noel."

He doesn't respond.

"Let's not go," I say.

He doesn't answer. "Seriously, Noel, let's not do this. Rick doesn't own us."

Noel sighs, "Yes, Jolette. Oh, yes, he does."

* * *

Ten minutes later, we disappear into another underground, unimposing Social Club. Noel keeps his gaze firmly on the ground. The Social Club is oppressively hot and overcrowded tonight and the whole bar area is sealed off.

There's an energy in the air. Hundreds of hedge fund managers rush through the hallways and Noel leads me into the elevator and we take it down to the basement.

Each area of the Society is equipped with sophisticated electronic surveillance systems that allow a centrally located guard in a control center to monitor what's happening in the entire facility.

Downstairs, we pass a guy who has two wrists tied to a chair. He's bleeding from his mouth, his forehead...

Dominic Black is punching him, and watching this is Paul Zucker. He grins, completely absorbed in this brutal showing of violence.

"Okay, Dominic! Stop! That's enough!" Noel shouts. He walks over to the young kid, unties his hands, and throws him his handkerchief.

The guy takes the handkerchief, and wipes the blood off his mouth and looks up at Noel."Noel, it's not my fault..."

Noel shakes his head. "You're through on the Street, Branson, you hear me?"

"Noel, wait!"

"We've been through this!"

"Nobody gets to Clayborn!"

"Those are the rules. Dominic, let him go."

Dominic steps back, lets him go. The broker stands, wobbles on his feet. "Noel, come on, don't do this."

"Get out of here!"

"I should have put a bullet in his fucking head," Dominic says.

Paul turns to Noel now, as I stand by watching this whole thing. "What are we going to do now?"

Noel stares at him without an answer and Rick announces over a loudspeaker, "Let's go everyone, the meeting is starting. Everybody needs to get downstairs. Take a seat now!"

Noel and I walk past a small indiscreet surveillance camera and rush in the main hall with the others. The trading systems are humming, running thousands of trades through and it's wall to wall people. There's a frenzied mood in the air.

Rick is up at the board. "Thank you, everyone, for coming. This is important or we wouldn't have called you out in the middle of the night. Prince Louieville the III, the rainmaker of Lichtenstein, is making a big play for the U.S. markets. He has access to a hundred billion dollar trust and he's a big player in crypto, NFT's in particular. He's ready to make a score, but first a few announcements.

"We want to congratulate Jolette Marco on getting our BSD award this month. Come on up here, Jolette!"

I look around, not expecting this.

The entire room starts clapping. Noel turns to me and smiles, nudging me to go up and get the award.

I step out of my chair, and hesitantly walk to the front. "Nice work," Rick says, and hands me a trophy.

I read the trophy: BSD: Big Swinging Dick. I'm mortified, but smile like I'm honored.

"Next," Rick continues, "I want to congratulate Noel Sheffield on getting approved on his transfer to the New York office. He'll be conducting his business from Rothman Securities' now out of New York — he's moving on with the big boys! Congratulations, Noel!"

Everyone starts clapping, and I sit back down, and turn to Noel and just stare at him.

Transfer? To New York?

When was he going to tell me this?

"If everybody remembers, Noel was responsible for the Triad's most profitable trade, the Bed, Bath and Beyond short, made earlier this year. He made the Society six hundred million on that play. Way to go, Noel!"

Everyone applauds.

Noel turns to me and smiles, guilty as charged.

My breath catches in my throat.

For a second, I cannot breathe.

I sit there watching everyone...and watching Noel...I study him as if I've never seen him before.

My face slowly takes on the overtones of a death mask; my green transparent eyes blaze with delirium, as I strive to control my anger.

"Guess your yacht can be twenty feet longer now, Sheffield!" a hedge fund guy says next to him.

The anguish in my body and soul is replaced with such a cold blooded rage that I want to strangle Noel with my bare hands.

I should have known he was responsible.

Master manipulator, Noel Sheffield.

That day I lost all of my father's money, Noel was behind it...

Two new names pop up on the screen and everybody turns back to Rick. "Okay, back to Prince Louisville the III. He plays big in a select few names. Four of our top lieutenants are working from the inside. They're pulling the trigger on LUNA and SHIB. We're going long. There's little float in both names, so they're going to move, and they're going to move fast. Also, we've got another rug pull on these select NFT's. The money's coming in, but we aren't delivering on anything."

There's smug laughter around the room. "Remember there's only three trading rules. Rule number 1: Don't lose money. Rule number 2: Don't forget rule number 1. And rule number 3: The only thing you should be holdin' overnight is your dick!"

A collective laugh rises in the air.

Rick adds, "Do not trade these stocks in your PA because when they start looking into activity, *and they will,* they'll come after you. Give the data to your *clients only*. Right now, commissions are the name of the game."

It appears as if everything starts moving in slow motion. I turn to the gated windows… and I see the first flicker of lights.

Then a flashlight…

I turn to another window, and I see *red lights flickering.* At first a few, then more.

Noel is clueless as my terrible, sinking feeling comes to life. And suddenly I realize…They're here. They're coming for us.

This place is getting raided.

The Club is going down...

Right now.

I see the first FBI uniform through the window…And then another…

I can't think.

I need to move, I need to *do something.*

They're coming in now, and they're going to bust this whole thing up. And I'm not going down with the ship. I whisper to Noel, "I need …to use the ladies room."

He gives me a look that says *don't YOU DARE get up and leave in the middle of Rick's speech,* but I don't care. I head for the ladies room, and once I'm inside, I hear it — the sound of pounding on the door. Then, it bursts open.

Then: the voices:"FREEZE, EVERYBODY! DON'T MOVE!"

Dozens, if not hundreds, of police and FBI officers break into the basement. Through the partially opened door, I see at least twelve helmeted FBI guys in uniform, the first members of the raiding party, rushing in.

It's utter pandemonium.

Hedge fund managers rush for the exit.

Any exit.

Dominic, the undercover informant, pulls out his police badge and hangs it around his neck as a half dozen cops line the hedge fund managers and brokers up against the wall. "Shut up!" Dominic commands.

Not a prayer.

"I said shut THE FUCK UP, GODDAMNIT!"

This quiets everyone.

"Under section 519 of the San Francisco Penal code, I serve notice that this premise and its occupants are under the exclusive control of the Federal Government and are subject to arrest."

Dominic handcuffs Noel and he's escorted out with the others.

Upstairs, in the back, Paul Zucker, plunges through an open window... Rick quickly runs for the Club's panic room, the secretive, insulated, bullet-proof room which monitors the Club from hundreds of cameras that nobody knows about.

Some of the hedge fund managers start to fight back, kicking and screaming, until the police order: "Get down on the ground!"

And one by one, they go down — chin to the pavement, handcuffed behind their back.

Terrified, I enter a bathroom stall and close the door. I see a loose ceiling panel and stand on the toilet, pushing it open and inside, I see an iron bar. I jump up and grab the bar, kicking my feet up, and hoist myself inside. I put the tile back over the hole and hold my breath.

I can hear my own breathing and the beat of my own heart. I hear the door of the ladies room get kicked open.

I don't move.

I close my eyes. The FBI kicks in the first stall door, then the second.

I'm frozen.

They're going to find me, *arrest me...* I hold my breath. *Oh, please, no.* They don't find me, and leave.

The whole raid doesn't take more than five minutes.

I climb down and the place is completely desolate. I exit the ladies room, slowly walk outside into the darkness, and the wail of police sirens can be heard in the distance.

I walk alone down the street still reeling and a van pulls up beside me. The back door slides open and Paul yells, "Get in, Jolette!" I turn and see Rick is driving.

Taking a drag off of his cigarette, he repeats, "Get in the fucking van, Jolette!"

I get in.

"What happened to Noel?" Rick asks, as he guns the engine and pulls away fast.

"They arrested him."

"Fuck!" He punches the steering wheel.

The van pulls up outside of ABLX Securities. People are heading into work.

"What are you doing?" I ask, "We can't do this!"

"What do you mean?" Rick counters. "It's business as usual. Go to work."

"But..."

"Go!"

I exit the van with a few of the others, and head inside ABLX Securities.

45

Chapter 45

I walk onto the trading floor… and my head is spinning. Looking around, I feel paranoid. *Does anybody know what just happened?*

I feel my cell phone vibrating.

Dare I answer it?

I look down at it, and father is calling. It's 4:50 in the morning. "Hi," I answer cautiously.

"Jolette, your brother has just admitted himself into rehab. I'm on my way there. I got a call in the middle of the night. He almost …died, Jolette." My father's voice cracks, "Can you come with me?"

"Now, Dad?"

"Yes, now."

I take a deep breath. "Sure, I'll meet you downstairs, what time?"

"I'm down here now. I'll wait for you."

"Okay."

My father and I head over to the rehab facility in silence. When we're almost there, he turns to me and asks, "How's everything, Jolette?"

I swallow. "Fine, Dad, everything's fine."

As he parks the car, he says, "Now we all had to do it. Her name is Dr. Friedman. She's a kind and patient woman. You'll enjoy speaking to her. After your mother died, Troy took it the hardest. He was her pride and joy..."

I nod.

"Tough Troy...all of his captivating B.S. I know you love him. But don't be afraid, Jolette, because you won't end up like him. He's made a mess of things, but you – you have some real strength in you. I see it every time I look at you."

I'm caught up in the heart of my father's decency.

"Go inside and I'll find a parking spot," he says.

I nod, and get out of the car. Moving toward the drab Rehab facility, I enter the building, and walk down a long corridor. I find the door that says Dr. Friedman, Counseling, and open it. The receptionist is not there. A clock says 6:10 a.m.

I see an inner door open, and when I walk in, I see my brother sitting on a couch.

Dr. Friedman, the rehab psychologist, is a very pretty dark-haired woman about forty years old. She's sitting across from my brother, and smiles. "How are you, Jolette?"

"I'm fine."

"Sit down," she says.

I sit down on the couch beside Troy. He puts his hand on my knee. "I've been sober five hours. I'm going to go to the meetings again. I just told Dad."

Troy sits there with a lethal smile and a shake he can't quite control anymore.

"That's good."

"Jolette, please, I know how bad I was. I want to make things right between us. Can you every forgive ... me?"

I look at him. A brick wall. "Sure. Forget it."

"Well, this is a great start," Dr. Friedman says."We are here to face the source of our traumas. Running to escape only makes solving them more difficult."

"The day our mom died, she made Jolette and Sarah wait in the car while she went inside the casino and gambled. She came out drunk and angry, crying because she lost the money. She didn't have any money left to buy our father a birthday gift..."

I look at my brother. I can't believe he's telling this story.

"So... Jolette suggested that they sell more Girl Scout cookies, you know, to get some of the money back. Jolette said she could triple the money... That's when Mom — ..."

He pauses. "That's when Mom started driving erratically and she crashed."

I listen and before I can realize, there's tears streaming down my face.

"And so our mother's last words to Jolette were, "You stupid girl, what do you know? Triple my money? I'm just a loser and so are you. And then she was dead."

I stare back at Troy and the therapist, in shock.

"I see. How does this make you feel, Jolette?" the therapist asks, turning to me.

How does she think it makes me feel? "I can't do this right now," I say. "I'm sorry, but I have to get back to work."

* * *

I arrive to the trading floor like a tiger coming home to the jungle, and sit down at my desk, and the ABLX Human Resources team is walking towards me.

"Is that them?" I hear Robbie ask Kimberly.

"Yep."

"Are they going to do it right here?"

"I think so," Kimberly answers, a malicious gleam in her eye.

"Fuck me," Robbie says, as they keep walking. "It's better to keep your head down. Just ignore it."

I watch them move closer wondering what is going on now. They stop in front of my desk. "Jolette Marco?"

"Yes?"

"Follow us, please."

I get up and they lead me into a conference room. I enter and ten managing directors are sitting around a conference table. Stacks of files are on that table.

Center stage is Monique. "Jolette, we have a situation."

I look around the room and see Jesus dressed in a suit, arms folded in his lap. "We found a massive trading error for Steve Benson hidden in an offshore account. I think you better come clean, Jolette," she says, "It's not going to be a problem, if you tell the truth."

"The truth...?" I ask, blindsided. "Monique instructed me to put the five million dollar Benson error in the 2007 Phi account."

"I don't know what she's talking about!" Monique banters.

"Why don't we go back to your office and get the files then?" I snap.

"She's lying!"

"Jolette, we can't find the files!" the HR rep informs the room evenly.

Monique asks harshly, "Did you *take* them, Jolette?"

"No, I didn't take them! Talk to Juan and Jesus in compliance!"

"We already spoke with Jesus," the HR rep responds, crisply.

I look around the room at a loss for words, and then I glance down at my watch.

"Is there someplace else you need to be, Jolette?"

I should have known this bitch would have crossed me, and after everything I've done for her... End of year bonuses are hanging in the air, and I should not even be surprised at this. The only thing worse than an enemy is a traitor. And Monique is the ultimate traitor. I am on the verge of total collapse.

After three hours of deliberations, I hear the words, "Jolette, your access to the building, computer systems, cell phone, American Express cards, and e-mail will be shut down immediately…You are terminated."

"Wait a minute!" But the guard takes my arm, and escorts me out of the conference room, and moves me across the trading floor.

I keep my head down as I walk, mortified as everybody stares at me.

The security guard guides me into the elevator and through the building lobby, and passing me are the traders from the morning carpool.

"Looks like I won't be needing a ride tomorrow, guys."

Their mouths gape open as they watch me exit ABLX Securities for the last time.

46

Chapter 46

Once I'm outside, I see that I have five text messages from Sarah. "It's Career Day! Did you forget?!"

There's a bunch of cabs parked outside on California Street, and I jump into the closest one, "St. John's elementary school! And please hurry!"

The driver nods, I look at my watch, wishing this car could go above the traffic and fly.

Traffic is horrendous, and we're barely moving.

I cannot miss this.

Cannot.

Once we hit VanNess, we start to move, and when the driver pulls up to the school, and I hand him my 'emergency' twenty, thank him, and jump out.

I rush toward the entrance…

There's a sea of children, all coming towards me. School is just letting out.

I push through them, rushing, trying to make it…. And then up ahead I see Sarah and the twins coming towards me.

Sarah looks at me and shakes her head.

Devin and Dan see me too.

I come toward them... And my heart is beating outside of my chest. *Please don't tell me that I missed their Career Day. Oh God, anything but that...*

I wave, smiling.

Everything's going to be okay, I tell myself.

But then, a black car pulls up beside me. And the another one. I turn around.

There's another.

And another.

I'm cornered.

Ten policemen are coming towards me.

I look back at Sarah.

And the twins.

One approaches... and I recognize the face... I recognize him ... *but from where?* "Jolette Marco, you have the right to remain silent..."

I see the handcuffs come out.

Oh, God, no. Not here.

My throat is so dry, I have to swallow before I can get the words out: "Please, not in front of my nephews."

The handcuffs tighten around my wrists. "Anything you say can and will be used against you in a court of law. You have the right to an attorney..."

I look up and see the looks on Devin and Dan's faces. Devin clutches his playing cards and holds the hand of his brother.

I feel the Officer's hand on my arm and with each breath, my heart feels like it's going to implode.

They stare at the police cars and watch as I am shoved down into the back of the police cruiser.

The door shuts.

I look out the window, and all the children are watching. I search

Sarah's eyes and they're blank.

She wraps her arms around the twins.

Devin starts to cry. She bends down, and says something to him. Whatever she's saying, doesn't seem to help. I see them nod.

Dan wraps his arm around his brother in consolation, staring at me through the police car window.

I lean back in the seat and struggle to catch my breath.

We drive off.

The looks on the twin's faces hurt more than any amount of money that I could ever lose in the stock market, or any amount of time that I will serve in prison.

A city bus passes us, and as I turn, I see Brittany's face, on the side of the bus in a Posh advertisement, smiling back at me.

47

Chapter 47

Menacing fluorescent lights and ten-foot high barbed wire fences surround the five story building. The officer gets out and opens the door, "Step out, please."

A female correctional officer comes out and nods. She looks me over and tells me to put my hands on the car and spread my legs. She pats me down and then walks me inside the facility.

We walk down a long corridor. Another San Francisco officer firmly leads me by my arm to a battered desk. "Empty your pockets on the desk."

I nod and do what I'm told. They ask for basic information and then I'm fingerprinted and photographed.

I'm lead down another long corridor. Every time the doors open taking me to another wing of this place, there are loud buzzing sounds. They seem to get louder and louder. The smell in here is horrendous. There is no air.

I pass a long line of women waiting at a window. Above the window is a sign: MEDS. They all stare at me. Their eyes hold nothing but remorse and coldness, and anger and hate. But what I can relate to is their hopelessness.

I'm shoved into a dimly lit cell and the door slams shut.

When I turn, the officer is gone.

Eighteen women are in this cell, lying on a slatted floor with no mattresses or blankets. It smells like dirty feet or urine, or both, and I'm instantly claustrophobic in this concrete cage that seems like it was made for animals.

An open toilet sits in the corner, and in another corner, I watch as a woman throws up all over the floor.

I drop to ground, numb.

This is a whole new low.

A whole new bottom.

I've always had a high tolerance for pain. But all thresholds have been smashed, bar none.

I have hit rock bottom.

This has to be the end of it. My habits have turned into death sentences. I have fallen into the abyss.

I have been completely and utterly defeated.

* * *

I wake up with blood caked on my face. It reminds me of the bomb. The bomb that went off in Noel's McLaren right before I left for New York. Even then, seconds away from being dead from an explosion – it didn't stop me.

I just kept moving forward.

And now here I lie on the floor in this jail in somebody else's vomit. I don't have the energy to move and I realize I have cashed in. This drive to be a trader, to hedge myself, over leverage myself, over and over and over again, has finally done me in.

Only this time, I can't go back and get a job. This time, I will have ruined my chances at getting a "regular job," which by now, I'd be grateful for. No, now I'll have a black mark on my record. A criminal mark. And this one will not fade.

Every hour of every day, the shadows of the guards show on the bars of the cell in this zoo of madness.

It occurs to me that I'm not getting out of here until somebody comes and lets me out.

I have tried to quit day trading. Once. Twice. A thousand times. Wall Street is a frenetic industry. And gambling is the hidden addiction. There is no smell, no tell-tale behavior, no white powder under the nose. It has a powerful allure and has always been my coping strategy. What started out so innocent became a fast plummet down a hazardous slope to financial and emotional ruin.

I never imagined how quickly it could all unravel. Or maybe I did.

I just didn't care.

Now my sense of self is degraded on every level.

I hear somebody scream. It's a psychotic, blood curdling scream. I look up and see somebody standing at the bars. I see a man in a police uniform and he is calling my name, I believe. I try to focus. I try to listen.

I slowly rise. I go closer to the bars. And who's standing there, but my father.

"Dad…"

I try to assess him but my eye is too swollen. I try to be strong. I want to tell him, "We're going to come back, Dad, we're going to get through this, *I have a plan. I will make. The. Money. Back. Dad. Really. I. Will."*

But all I do is break down, first some tears, then sobs. I know he hates it when I cry.

I know he never can find the right words to comfort me.

But I can't help it. "I'm sorry, Dad…. I never realized anything like this could happen…"

He holds up his hand, stopping me. "Jolette. I don't want to see you doing this to yourself."

I bite my lower lip, "…I have made some terrible mistakes…"

He nods as though my words make sense. "You learned from the past, now try to recapture the things you think you lost. Don't make the same mistakes again and move forward. I'm behind you all the way."

"You really mean that, Dad?"

"Yes, Jolette. You're doing what I've always done. Chasing fame, fortune, money, power, the externals. I've had all those things. Seek happiness from within or you will never find it…"

A faint hope appears on my face. My father reaches out for my hand. "Integrity will always be your richest asset."

"I can't believe you would forgive me, Dad," I say, clutching at him, crying unashamedly, as his words envelop me.

The guards says my father has to leave.

He kisses my forehead through the bars. "I love you," he says, with tears in his eyes.

And then he goes.

48

Chapter 48

Days pass. I've been placed on another floor and am housed in Jail #4. It's a traditional linear jail located on the 7th floor of the Hall of Justice. The whole place is sealed off.

Deputy Sheriffs monitor all inmate activity and patrol the cells on each side of the central corridor.

Over the coming days, I grasp the criminal justice system intimately. It's a closed Society, as secret in its operations as the Triad. It's a microcosm of the larger world outside though much more volatile and dangerous. "You pussy-ass bitch," my cell mate says to me on a constant basis.

I'm a pariah of society and I absolutely cannot stand it. This is home for humanity's absolute worst, and to survive here, even amongst the staff, is to compete daily for the chance to live.

In the five days that I've spent in this cell, not one officer has come in to explain my status.

I have a hard time with the constant company of the other prisoners whose history and behavior I cannot predict. Death is better than this, I think.

"Marco! Are you ready? Follow us!"

I rise. I hear them unlock those doors, those doors, those buzzing sounds...

I follow the guards through the jail, and outside, across the street, into another building.

We enter a conference room and there are ten policemen standing there and a team of what looks like attorneys. They are dressed in business suits, all in their mid-fifties.

I'm seated, and they take out a pair of handcuffs and attach one to my wrist and the other to the arm of the chair.

The door opens again and in walks... someone I recognize again, but from where?

Now I remember. He's the guy from the airport. The airport restaurant.

"Hello again, Jolette," he says. "Remember me? I'm FBI Agent Cullen Steele."

I don't say anything.

"How are you feeling?"

He stares at me. "Ms. Marco. May I call you Jolette? Do you know who it is that you're in business with? As you now know, I'm with the Department of Justice. We've been conducting this investigation for the past three years. Have you heard of a Ponzi scheme? "

I nod.

"It's run by a central operator who uses monies from new incoming investors to pay off the promised returns to older investors. The operation seemed profitable and legitimate. You see, his investing strategies were vague and secretive. People were encouraged to stay in the game to earn even more money..."

He keeps speaking and I'm trying to figure out where he's going with this. I don't even know who he's talking about.

"It's not just fat cat billionaires and celebrities he bilked... Hundreds of retail investors, banks, even charities lost money in the scheme.

This guy was a real Wall Street player, a financial wizard, a man who made a lot of people a lot of money… But things began to deteriorate earlier for Steve Benson this year when clients began requesting twenty billion back in returns, but he only had five hundred million left to give."

Steve. *Benson? What?*

"Because Mr. Benson was so active and well-versed in the financial industry, it's hard to believe he knew exactly what he was and is doing, but trust us, Jolette, he does. By the end of this month, we'll be uncovering his $300 billion dollar Ponzi scheme. He's responsible for a three hundred billion dollar cave in."

My mouth gapes open. "Billion with a B?"

He nods. "That's right, billion with a B."

I'm staggered.

I sit silently for several seconds, absorbing this news. "So get indictments and uncover it," I say, weakly.

"No. We need someone on the inside, someone with access to bank account numbers, routing numbers. According to the documents filed in the case, you set up the Bernstein account when you were with ABLX Securities and conspired with Benson to conceal his affiliation."

Omigod. How did they know?

"The FBI received tips after obtaining several piles of incriminating documents from Benson's private island in Romania. Your old brokerage firm is the sole rep and the investors are streamlined by your old boss, Monique Levine. She's set up legitimate trades with dirty money. All cash. And it's all moved offshore."

I stare at Cullen — stunned — paralyzed –

"Benson has a very good front – probably forty percent of his clients are legit. You need to tell us what you know, Jolette. And you better tell us now"

An attorney starts speaking, "The U.S. Securities & Exchange

Commission has lodged civil charges against you and 1,300 other people, uncovering the largest, most extensive insider trading scandal ever uncovered on Wall Street. The criminal charges against you include, but are not limited to: securities fraud, conspiracy, wire fraud, and insider trading. You're currently facing a possible sentence of up to ten years in prison and a $50 million dollar fine."

"For your cooperation," Cullen continues, "we'll grant you immunity. As a CI, or Confidential Informant, we'll dismiss your charges. You're familiar with bank accounts, wiring numbers, and that's what we need. We need people who have the "in" with Benson, and you certainly do. Once you're on the inside, you'll be able to provide us with copies of client statements, wiring instructions, bank records…"

On the inside?

Inside of what?

I don't want to be inside anymore. Of anything...

Cullen glances around and then his eyes settle on my face. "If you help us, Jolette, we'll make it worth your while, we'll protect you."

"Protect me?"

"We'll incorporate all the normal steps and safeguards due to the inherent risks in undercover informant work. We'll provide you with wiretaps…a government issued cell phone, laptop… It's in the strong interest of the FBI to keep you safe."

I'm so stunned, I can hardly think.

A thousand thoughts topple over one another. "To keep me safe?" I ask, as the reality of this begins to dawn in my eyes.

He nods.

I turn away.

"How long will it take for you to figure out that your boyfriend, Noel Sheffield, is testifying against you in the insider trading case?"

I turn back sharply and stare at Cullen, "What?"

I don't hear anything after that.

Later, they tell me I fainted.

49

Chapter 49

That winter the snow came very late. Cullen Steele and Dominic Black had pounced on a cheap room west of Columbus Circle in New York City.

They established a command post there to monitor the comings and goings of myself and other employees of Benson LLC. They requested a meeting with me as soon as possible. I told them no. I was too busy. Maybe next week, was all I said.

* * *

I moved into one of Benson's vast corporate penthouses high above Central Park. I took him up on that job he offered me and my subsidized castle in the sky afforded every amenity. It had an aristocratic interior, inlaid marble floors, stately columns, gold draperies and crystal chandeliers. It even had a private slide that lead directly down into an infinity pool.

Benson said I could stay in his "corporate housing," for as long as I needed to and he placed me in his Operations division. The leverage and power that he sustained all over the Street was incomprehensible.

And I was a part of it now. I was a part of Benson's esteemed organization.

The club everybody wanted to get into – Benson LLC — and even some of the best didn't qualify.

His headquarters occupied forty floors of prime office space in the heart of Rockefeller Center and the place vibrated around the clock with the chaos that came from the traders and junior traders.

This was where the hot traders worked. A gleaming testament to power. The sheer power and size of this place was enormous, and it was a sheer octopus of an organization with tentacles that stretched out all around the world.

With my role in operations, I was put in charge of handling all the monies coming in and out of the firm. I learned a lot, I was working around the clock, and I was obtaining a massive amount of data for the Feds.

For who would have ever guessed, myself included, that once the curtain was pulled, the till would be empty.

* * *

Standing in front of Benson's Xerox machine, it cranks out high-speed copies, twelve pages a second, and all the paperwork is a blur to me. The only constant is the firm logo: BENSON LLC as copies of client statements, trade confirmations, and other privileged documentation goes through.

As I take notice of some of the dates on some of the documents, I can't believe that Benson was able to get away with this for this long.

But once you're at Benson's level, you can do whatever you want. The SEC and every other agency magically transforms into a personal harem, including politicians who also become willing prostitutes.

Slowly, carefully, I was putting together the documentation that would lead to his descent and the screws would be put to him soon. I posted a question to Cullen: We could tape him tonight, burn this whole operation down to the ground overnight." But he wanted to do it his way.

Fine.

With each uneventful day, I withdrew more into my asylum. My world lapsed into a grey matter of nothingness without any organic meaning. Working for Benson now, and under the strict direction of the Feds, I had no contact or connection anywhere.

I even had to leave my cat behind. Troy said he would take care of him. It was a part of his "amends."

I glance up at the TV in the copy room. It's playing the evening news and I see Noel coming out of a courtroom.

"The U.S. Securities and Exchange Commission suffered a loss today when a jury cleared a San Francisco hedge fund manager and twenty others accused of engaging in a 11.3 billion dollar insider trading scheme...The jury found Noel Sheffield, an institutional broker with Rothman Securities, not liable on any insider trading charges."

I watch as the news media chase Noel down the street, trying to obtain a statement.

The newscaster continues, "Noel Sheffield hugged his lawyer after the verdict was read, and later on, outside of the courtroom, he criticized the SEC for engaging in an overreaction of regulatory overreach. He promised to push for policy changes to ensure this doesn't happen again."

Noel is grabbed for an interview. He looks into the camera, bright eyed, and calm. "There's no better use of one's wealth than to clean one's own reputation," he says, and walks off.

The newscaster continues, "His attorney told us earlier he was looking forward to getting on with his life, and a spokesman for the SEC said the agency was disappointed but respected the verdict... In other financial news…"

I shake my head.

I thought he loved me.

Imagine if he hated me.

* * *

I go back to my desk and look around and find five portable flash drives in my desk. I slide one into the USB port on the back of my computer, and then I copy a bunch of files to the drive. I decide to pour all the Sequenom stock into one master account. Benson still has massive quantities.

I pick up my cell, "Cullen are you there?"

"What is it?"

"Oh my God," I say softly.

"What is it?"

"We're screwed, Cullen."

"What are you talking about?"

I pretend to see images of myself on the screen in front of me. "I'm looking at photos of myself that are taken from security cameras and the quality of the shots are good enough for Benson to ID me."

"What?"

"Yes. Photos! Of me taking files. Making copies. Leaving. They've got it all on tape, Cullen!"

"They're onto us, Dominic," I hear Cullen say, "We need to do this now!" Back into the phone, he screams to me, "Fucking split, now, Jolette! That's a goddamn order!"

"I'm gone," I respond.

50

Chapter 50

Sheets of freezing rain raps the window and my preparations are now officially complete. I'm in a town car going over to Benson's private Holiday lunch soiree that he's hosting for some of his elite clients at his Manhattan Upper East Side penthouse.

I listen to the ice rain splatter against the window. The driver sees a bum on the street. "Bet that guy has more money than you and me both. They don't fool me."

I can't help but grin. I mean, after everything. "It's never as it seems, is it?"

The driver pulls up outside of Benson's 5th Avenue town home. I enter, and my coat is taken.

As I make my way inside, I see Daniel Lutz at a podium…I watch him from afar with a clear sense of unmistakable danger and power.

I know the undercover agents are following me. They are forced to get within twenty meters of me for my protection. I wonder if they are able to get in here, as Daniel starts to speak. "His name has become legend. His hedge fund is unprecedented. Without a doubt, one of the most successful men alive in the financial community today, I give you… Steven Benson."

Three hundred of Wall Street's elite are seated around tables for this elaborate lunch. Loud applause rings out.

Steve Benson approaches the podium, taking in the applause. I applaud, smiling.

Some of Benson's light spills onto me.

When he starts speaking, I slip out a side door and walk briskly down a long hallway.

I pass from one room to the next, and all of the austere, tastefully decorated rooms blend together. I'm looking for Benson's office and a series of immense, square rooms flow into each other through high triangular arches reminiscent of medieval monastic architecture.

Shiny chandeliers drop down from domed ceilings like giant stalactites. A cool breeze wafts its way inside, carrying with it the reminder of my master plan.

It's airtight.

And nothing better go wrong...

I start into one room, back up, go into another. I'm lost, getting frantic. I double back and cut toward another wing of the house.

Finally, sitting at Benson's work station, I slip a CD-ROM into his PC. It floods with account numbers and balances.

Hunched over the computer, I type commands into the keyboard. I begin selling Benson's Sequenom shares, getting him out at the high of the day. Sequence after sequence of coded numbers flash past on the monitor screen. After I blow him out of his position by fifty percent, the stock begins tanking.

With the cash, I begin buying back the stock. I put a million trades through the systems; hundreds of thousands of little trades…all buying Sequenom. So many trades all in the discretionary accounts. Nothing can drop this thing once Benson started buying it. Seventy billion dollars worth of cash was what I have access to…

And the stock begins rising…*fast.*

I had heard through some of my connections that Rick did actually go the other way on Sequenom. He went short.

Rick and the Society were short and counting on Sequenom going to 10. They were going to knock it back down.

But too bad now motherfuckers.

Looks like its game over. You will all be vaporized now. I hit up the stock message boards: "BUY SEQUENOM NOW! WHALE BUYER. ALL RETAIL BUY AND HOLD!!!"

I push speed dial on my cell phone and hear Rick's voice. "Don't you have a stock to manipulate, you creepy bastard?"

I keep hitting the keys, more trades, more of Benson's orders going through the system. It's going to be a death spiral for him, for the Society! All I have to do is trip up Rick and the rest will come tumbling down. And once I set this goal in motion, nothing will deter me from achieving it.

Rick can't understand what is happening. His voice quivers as the attack continues."Geesus! Oh God!"

He panics and his net worth is disintegrating right before his very eyes. How well do I know *that feeling*. It's a runaway train and every second that he doesn't cover, he's out millions.

"How does it feel to be left holding the bag, Rick?"

I stare into the computer. Eyes blazing.

In a clear, light voice, I say, "Looks like you should cover, Rick. Take the hit," I continue frostily. "Stock's rising like a fucking tornado."

The reality overwhelms him, and with dawning horror, he understands the truth.

I'm burying him. "What are you doing, Jolette? Get Benson to sell the stock! Unload it!"

"I'd rather see you suffer, Rick. And besides, I am Benson now."

He stutters, "Youuu ....you're Benson?"

"I trade his capital now!"

"How is that possible?"

"I call the shots now!" I cry, almost hysterical.

Thinking I hear something, I look up. Nobody is there.

* * *

Panicked, now over Skype, I see Rick jump up from his desk. He moves quickly, erratically around the office, and then back to his computer. He's frantic, and the clamor of the clicker is drowning out his thoughts like an exploding freight train. "Listen to me, Jolette…You sell your portion of this! RIGHT NOW!"

He's realizing the truth: I smashed his life.

And all of my anger slips away with every dollar Rick is losing… "You listen to me, YOU COCKSUCKER! Whoever has the leverage has the power! And I have the power now! DO YOU HEAR ME?! I HAVE THE POWER NOW!"

I sit in front of the computer going crazy and keep punching more buttons on the keyboard, manipulating the stock with Benson's massive buy orders.

Rick, in defeat, cues up 1,200,000 SQN shares… BUY TO COVER @ 94.10. LOSS - $93,538,393.

I watch him over Skype as his eyes swim with terror. "Do you remember that day you and your *Society* manipulated Bed, Bath and Beyond, Rick? I will never forget that day. And now, neither will you."

My face is a bronze mask, my eyes, deadly as steel, and Rick stares back at me, thunderstruck.

"You're gonna pay for this, Marco, do you hear me – we know where you live! We know where your family lives…!" and as he continues his rant, I hit the "play" button on my high tech recording device that's so generously provided to me by the FBI.

I remove my glasses, rub my eyes, and watch as Sequenom goes higher and higher, and Rick continues his violent tirade of threats—which will ultimately bury him, if this Sequenom trade doesn't.

* * *

Cullen and Dominic look at each other from their command post, concerned. "I can't hear anything, can you?"

"No. Check the sound!" Cullen orders."Jolette, where are you?! Answer now!"

"Where is she?" I hear Dominic ask incredulously.

You see, the Feds had videotapes of Benson's office. That whole place was tapped. But not his home. They could not see what I was up to at his home…

That's one for the team...

51

Chapter 51

Concentrating, I don't see anyone in the doorway. Finally, the numbers recede on the screen. After a moment, I sense something or someone is there. I don't breathe.

When I look up, Benson is standing in the doorway.

He enters his office and comes toward me, his enmity more palpable than ever. "You focus on the big picture, Jolette," he says. "But somewhere down the chain, something breaks down. Something or someone gets destroyed. At first it's devastating. You feel as if you've lost control."

He crosses the room, locks eyes with mine.

"You trade billions of dollars at a clip. You do something other people could never do. They lack the imagination, the nerve, the risk. But that's who you are."

Benson reads the screen. It's filled with text, whatever I loaded when I sat down.

"But you've become a barracuda in the process. And if you stay at this any longer, you'll become worse than I am."

He sits down. Spent.

"You see, Jolette, the rewards were never just about the money.

People found me brilliant, they depended on me. I'm a wise man and people need to be around me. But I'm not the only one who got what they needed. Because my clients, at the same time — they got what they needed too. They got rewards and security. Isn't that what you seek, Jolette? Security, predictability, certainty?"

I don't say anything.

"Isn't it?"

I nod.

"Well, for that, my clients looked away. They ignored the warning signs — those remarkable earnings. They saw simply what they wanted to see…"

He turns away and walks toward the bar, pours himself a scotch. "I really believed that I was just one good week away in trading and I'd make it all back."

I mumble, "Sociopath," under my breath.

He hears it. "We live in a society that rewards sociopaths. Don't we? We rise easily through corporate America, unchallenged, unstoppable, unscrutinized. The qualities that make us succeed are the very ones that ensure what's best for ourselves and our corporate entities."

"Creating disasters for mankind as a whole."

"What I did is no different than compulsive gambling — you double and triple down during a losing streak, hoping your luck will change. But it never does. You become so deep in the hole that you can never recover…"

I understand him too well. Maybe we are more alike than I think.

"So you begin to rationalize. *Everything.* By day, I robbed my friends blind; by night, I attended their charity balls and bathed myself in their accolades. We were caught because of the unknown variable, the market downturn. It's the one thing that will always bring us down."

Benson sits down, tired. "But don't be fooled, Jolette. I don't think any of my clients will be cutting back on their lifestyles any time soon.

They'll still be vacationing in the South of France, buying overpriced artwork and attending their magnificent charity balls to see and be seen..."

"Why did they blindly trust you?"

"Simple. The basic human desire to believe in something that's too good to be true. This goes all the way back to the beginning of time starting with the notion of Santa Claus. When it comes to the upper class, what drives them, what they really desire most is the feeling to "belong." In a world dominated by exclusive country clubs and private parties, the desire not to be left out is so overwhelming that it clouds the judgment of all but the most confident rich-man..."

I nod. "Do the right thing, Mr. Benson. End this. Turn yourself in."

Benson's guard walks in. "Everything okay Mr. B?"

Benson shakes his head. "No."

The guard pulls out a gun.

* * *

Cullen and Dominic sit at the console listening over headsets from a van outside.

"What the hell is she doing?" Dominic asks.

"You should have put a camera in there... She's in danger!"" Cullen shouts into a cell phone. "Go move in! Go in! Now!"

* * *

Outside, eight men jump out of the van and head inside with guns — Emergency. Cullen's announcement sports the urgency level by a hundred percent and the men crash into Benson's town home, pushing past people and investors —

"Get your hands up! — NOW! NOW! HANDS UP!"

They rush upstairs, find Benson, and enter the room.

Benson turns — raises his hands —

The voices move closer. "Turn around slowly!"

Then another voice, "DON'T MOVE OR I'LL BLOW YOUR HEAD OFF!"

I turn around slowly as two FBI guys, guns drawn, come through the open door.

* * *

Outside, another Helicopter lands on top of the rooftop —

Cullen and Dominic are already flooding in — like Marines —

"Put the gun down! Put it down!"

Benson's guard drops the gun, Cullen walks around and puts handcuffs on Benson. He stares at me, not even surprised, he knew this was coming.

I just shake my head.

* * *

I'm airlifted away in the helicopter.

Cullen and two other FBI agents, rip the tape off my chest, retrieving a small tape recorder.

Benson's voice is played back on the tape: "We rise easily through corporate America..."

"You did the right thing, Jolette. You just helped a lot of people."

52

Chapter 52

I called Sarah before I left New York and I'm hoping she'll be at the airport in San Francisco to pick me.

She's probably still mad at me and she has every right to be. I have no idea what I'm coming home to but when I come through the airport gate, and I make my way through the crowd, I see a media frenzy.

Cameramen. Newscasters. Photographers.

And right in front of them, waiting for me, is my family.

My father. Troy. Sarah. Her husband. The twins. Brittany. All standing there. Smiling.

I'm shocked.

I grin and pick up speed as cameras start to go off… And I bury myself in my sister's arms hugging her. "You're a hero, Jolette," she says.

"What?" I turn.

"Jolette, how does it feel to save forty percent of the investors of Steve Benson's hedge fund?"

I look into a camera…stunned… and look back at my family who moved aside as the news reporters move in.

Someone from CNBC speaks first, "We are standing here with Jolette Marco, an Institutional Broker previously with ABLX Securities who helped the Feds in securing back 220 billion dollars for investors by locating the money that Benson had hidden in offshore accounts, and then she traded it buying Sequenom which was this weeks stock winner, up another 30% on high volume... How'd you do it, Jolette?"

I take a deep breath, as someone else asks, "Any plans to run your own hedge fund now, Ms. Marco?"

"No."

"Why is that?"

"Because it's not a fair playing field. It's not fair to the little guy... and I guess in the end...I'll always just be a little guy."

I turn, and with my family, stride out of the airport.

The TV anchorwoman continues to speak into the camera: "And that ends Steve Benson's three hundred billion dollar Ponzi scheme and the insider trading ring that brought three hundred people to justice.

In a related story, Paul Zucker, Wall Street's renown ABLX Securities analyst has committed suicide, apparently another victim of Steve Benson's Ponzi scheme. Next, we'll be interviewing some of the victims. People who have lost everything, including an eighty year old woman now living out of a trailer in Florida. Stay tuned."

53

Chapter 53

I approach the twins sitting on the dock. They're observing a Western sky that's turning peach and sapphire.

I sit down next to them. "Remember… how I used to trick you with those magic tricks?"

Devin's small, skinny arms go around my neck, nuzzling against me affectionately. They nod.

"Well, I tricked some people in my job…for money. Because I thought money would give me freedom, but when we do bad things we are never free in here." I point to my head and my heart.

"And this hurts and everything hurts… and then you get in trouble, and you have to be punished and apologize. I'm so sorry I missed your Career Day…"

The twins watch me.

They still hold an expression of such trust in their eyes.

"And from now on, Aunt Jolette always does the right thing, okay?"

I bend over to kiss them and press back against the tears that are coming no matter what I do.

* * *

Our sleepy little town…in Tiburon California. I went from a $3000 outfit to a T-shirt and jeans. I sit around a table at a restaurant celebrating Father's Day with my family. I hand him a card.

"Thank you," he says.

"Open it."

My father opens the envelope and pulls out a check. It's all of his retirement money back. He grins.

"I won't be trading anymore, Dad." I smile at him, beaming.

"Good."

Sarah pulls me close and hugs me.

My father looks at me with love and pride, and finally, complete understanding of what I've been going through from the beginning.

I look at Troy over Sarah's shoulder, and smile, with tears in my eyes.

* * *

I have been seeing Troy's therapist privately. I liked her a lot and was making headway. "I haven't placed a trade in over eight months," I tell her during one of our sessions. "On bad days, I just want to numb out. But somebody once told me that day trading was a hard way to make an easy living. I try to remember that and where it brought me. My new friends help me, and the glass is no longer half empty. It's half full. And I have a lot to be grateful for."

* * *

Brittany and I did the Triathlon later that year. We didn't win, but we finished. And I was okay with that.

* * *

I work at a restaurant now; at a tiny café in Tiburon, and I'm a waitress. It doesn't pay well, but I get by and I enjoy interacting with the customers. They're really nice people. I feel different. Happy, serene.

As I fix a milkshake for a little boy, he asks, "Is this enough, Miss?" He pulls out five dollars. "I think I am short twenty-five cents."

I smile. "Let me see."

Suddenly a quarter is placed down on the table.

I look up and it's Noel. In a suit. Looking magnificent. "Hi."

* * *

Noel and I walk down a tree lined street. "I just wanted somebody to talk to."

"...About what, Noel?"

"We have a lot of history. And you have reasons to be mad. I'm sorry about everything."

We smile at each other. Okay. Friends even.

"It's good to hear that," I say, "I'm willing to close that chapter and move on."

"Well, I'm not willing to do that. I can't stop thinking about you."

He hands me an envelope. "I wanted to bring you this. It's an invitation, for this Saturday..."

* * *

Back at ABLX Securities, there aren't any more Benson files to guard, but the traders are screaming...And Monique, "GET MOVING

PEOPLE! TIME IS MONEY!

I hear her new assistant has been going crazy, juggling the phones, sitting in the place that I used to sit.

54

Chapter 54

It's one of those days when the San Francisco Bay sparkles like a glitter ball. The sky is blue and cloudless, the sun bright.

I step out of a taxi.

Walking along the marina of the Clipper Yacht Harbor, I hear a Bell-Boeing 609 tilt-roter helicopter appear in the sky. Everybody looks up and watches as the helicopter lands, and Noel steps off.

I watch him from afar.

He's back. So very, very back.

His yacht is beyond huge; it's the Arioso on steroids. But beyond that, is an even bigger yacht: "The Maltese."

I wait against a railing, and Noel approaches.

He looks better than ever. Stronger than ever. *And* more confident. If *that's even possible.* His hair is perfect, his skin luminous, and he simply, positively glows. "Looks like you're back," I say.

Noel looks down on me with an indolent amusement. He begins talking so fast, moving so fast, then he points not to his yacht, but The Maltese. "You see that yacht over there? Someday mine's going to be bigger than that."

He's repeating the exact same words he said to me over a year ago.

As if nothing has changed.

Noel takes my hand. "I'm half owner of that now," he announces. We move closer to his yacht.

I let go of his hand....and look back to — *what?*

"What are you doing?" he asks, and then he grins, "We're going to Cannes. I have fifty million, we can start our own fund..."

I look at the yacht. At him. And the long narrow pathway that leads me out of the Marina.

"Jolette, you need to be here. With me."

"I can't trade, Noel. Period."

"You lost a little bit of money. Once..."

"Two million."

"And that buys you a waitress job for the rest of you're life? You're better than that. Come on! Everything's changing!"

I look back at the yacht. At him. And the long pier behind me.

On the yacht, Rick and Thomas look through the glass, riveted, watching Noel and I on the marina.

"I have a life, now, Noel."

"Who — what? *Your dad?* The other waitresses? They're nobody."

"If they are. Then I am."

"Marry me, Jolette."

I look at him — shocked. I laugh, then suddenly, I begin to weep. I repeat the same words that Sarah once said to me, "The four most dangerous words in investing and in life are, "'This time it's different.'"

Noel reaches for my hand, but I pull away fiercely, shielding my face, crying.

"Jolette, we can start over. We can live anywhere. We can be happy together."

I laugh, sadly, long past this kind of fantasy.

"You don't want to come, do you?"

"I do," I reply. "But not with you."

This hits Noel hard.

He looks away, his eyes moist.

I smile gently.

Our eyes met. And lock.

"You know, it's not the money I love Jolette, but the control. There's a thousand different women out there; different faces, different bodies, but the one thing, the one person, I could never control, was you."

"What? You controlled me in a thousand different ways, Noel. You pulled me in a million different directions… you…"

I stare at him, looking for words.

But none come.

We share a moment of understanding.

I nod my head, in thanks and in farewell.

Noel doesn't react. He turns and steps onto the yacht. He takes a seat on board as a beautiful woman in a tight sheath of an evening dress approaches. "Noel?"

Noel turns away, distracted. "…Hey…" he replies.

And he turns, watching me…walking away.

I look back at him again.

And then I turn away slowly, from the yacht, and all that life represents.

My gaze rises as I walk, looking forward.

In the end, I guess I got what I always wanted. I stopped. I stopped trading. *And it was done.*

The sounds of the party around me began to fade away. And moment by moment, a certain relief takes over.

I keep moving… with a subtle, but undeniable flicker of hope and determination in my eyes.

The End.

About the Author

Juliana Jones started her career at Robertson Stephens working in the Venture Capital Distribution group, was promoted to Institutional Sales, and then transferred to New York where she was hired at Morgan Stanley as a Senior Vice President. She ended her career at Carlin Financial, the firm talked about in Michael Lewis' financial thriller Flash Boys.

Currently, she is Chief Investment Strategist, Proprietary Trading Account, Citygirl Holdings. ❤ Volatility trader. 💰 She day trades and then taste lattes ☕ around the world.

You can connect with me on:

- https://citygirllovescoffee.com
- https://twitter.com/citygirlj
- https://facebook.com/citygirlj7
- https://www.instagram.com/citygirljuliana
- https://amzn.to/3q8hjB3
- https://www.amazon.com/author/citygirlj

Subscribe to my newsletter:

- https://citygirllovescoffee.com/contact

Also by Juliana Jones

Does Jolette really stop trading? And is this the end of her and Noel? Find out in the next book:

THE VALENTINE'S DAY CONCERT
She ropes a Hollywood playboy into going to the concert in Las Vegas on Valentine's Day. What could possibly go wrong?

www.ingramcontent.com/pod-product-compliance
Lightning Source LLC
LaVergne TN
LVHW100258210926
848480LV00003B/954
* 9 7 9 8 9 8 5 3 2 2 4 0 8 *